1986

NOT WITHOUT STRUGGLE

The Story
of
William E. Hoy
and the
Beginnings of Tohoku Gakuin

by
C. William Mensendiek

With a Foreword by
President Tetsuo Seino

Tohoku Gakuin, Sendai, Japan
1986

All rights reserved
© 1986 Tohoku Gakuin

Printed by
Sasaki Printing & Publishing Co., Ltd.
Sendai, Japan

William E. Hoy (1885)

Hoy's Birthplace

Hoy's Home Church

Hoy's article in The Messenger, Nov. 29, 1882

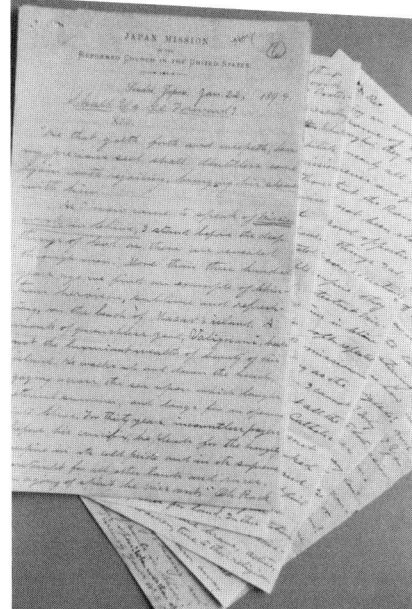

Hoy's letter, Jan. 22, 1899

Rudolph F. Kelker

Emma & Lizzie Poorbaugh,
Anna & David Schneder,
Jairus & Annie Moore, Kittie Poorbaugh,
William & Mary Hoy (upper right)
Kittie Poorbaugh (about 1888)

The Gring Family (about 1886)

Hoy and Oshikawa with first students (about 1886)

The first meeting of Miyagi (Sendai) Classis (about 1886)

John Ault Memorial Hall (built in 1888)

The Seminary Building (built in 1893)

Sendai Church (built in 1901)

Industrial Home Students

The Hoy Family (about 1896)

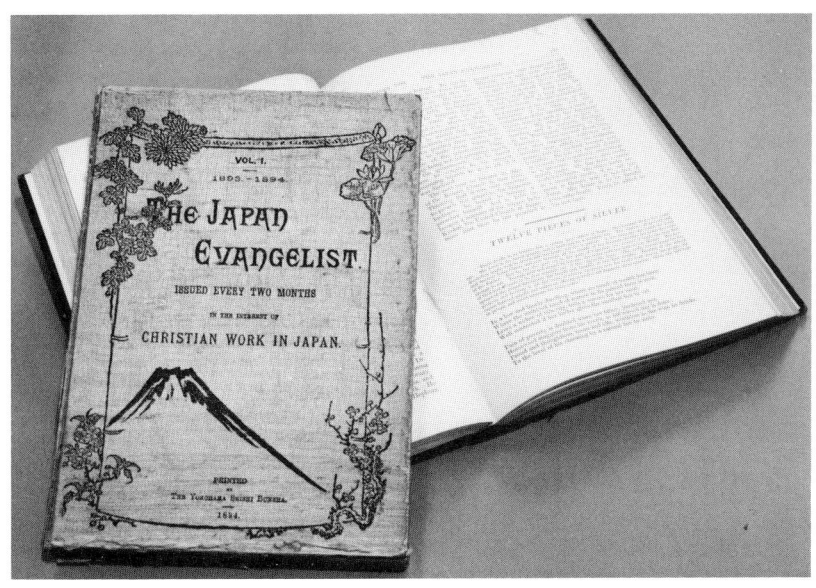

The Japan Evangelist (1893)

The Hoy Farewell (1899)

View of Lakeside Schools from Tungting Lake

Hoy at Lakeside School, Yochow

Lakeside School Chapel

The Chapel today

Mensendiek at Lakeside School (1984)

William Hoy Memorial in Sendai, Japan   Mary Hoy grave in Hankow, China

William Hoy grave in Mifflinburg, Pennsylvania

Tohoku Gakuin Campus today

PREFACE

With the centenary of the founding of Tohoku Gakuin coming next year, I am more than happy to know that the biography of Rev. William E. Hoy, one of the founders of the school, has been completed by Dr. William Mensendiek, professor of Tohoku Gakuin.

Prior to his second term of service in Japan, Dr. Mensendiek received his doctor's degree for his research in the missionary work in foreign countries, and after returning to Sendai he wrote, "A Man for His Times: The Life and Thought of David Bowman Schneder, Missionary to Japan, 1887-1938," who was our second president. This volume made a deep impression not only on the late President Tadao Oda and many other alumni but also on the people who were interested in the history of education in Christian schools in Japan.

Dr. Mensendiek has since been continuing his investigation of the lives and works of his missionary predecessors, digging into and digesting a great deal of source material both in this country and in the U.S. In his devotion to every detail he even visited China where the Hoys, because of William's health problem in Japan, were transferred at the turn of the century to pioneer Christian work in Hunan.

In 1956 it was proposed by some alumni volunteers to build, as one of the projects of the 70th Anniversary of the founding of the school, a monument for Rev. Hoy, together with a tomb for Dr. Teizaburo Demura, the third president. The unveiling ceremony took place at Kitayama, Sendai, in front of the tombs of the Schneder family on the 15th of April. There was a large attendance, and all were happy that they had with them Miss Gertrude Hoy, the eldest daughter of Rev. Hoy, who was then a missionary teacher at Miyagi Women's College. In answer to the request to make a short speech, the sixty-year-old lady said something like this: "Thank you very much for the kindness you have shown in memory of my father. But excuse me for speaking frankly. I am afraid my father would not be pleased with this stone monument. For it is not stone but people like Dr. Demura, Dr. Oda, Mr. Tsukiura and many others from Tohoku Gakuin who can commemorate him." This was a little surprising to me, but soon I realized that it was like the famous Gettysburg Address. It seemed to have deeply moved the former pupils of the late Vice-president Hoy, among whom I am not numbered. During the past thirty years since then, Miss Hoy and those whom she named who were my seniors have all passed away. Although Miss Hoy's words are still ringing in my ear, the monument to Rev. Hoy seems to talk about the unforgettable existence of the great founder of our school. I wish to think that the building of the monument was full of meaning.

It seems to me that the completion of the Hoy life story has put life into that monument at Kitayama. If Miss Gertrude Hoy were alive she would say, "I am sure my father would be pleased with this book."

We are planning to send this book to the United States, hoping that it will be welcomed by the friends of Tohoku Gakuin University, formerly called North Japan College.

Tetsuo Seino, President

Sendai, June 1985.

TABLE OF CONTENTS

Preface	–	Dr. Tetsuo Seino
Photographs		
Introduction		 i
Chapter I	–	Beginnings in Pennsylvania 1
Chapter II	–	Beginnings in Japan 16
Chapter III	–	Beginnings in Sendai 29
Chapter IV	–	Beginning Imperatives 47
Chapter V	–	Beginning of Creative Tensions 65
Chapter VI	–	Beginning of Reaction 92
Chapter VII	–	Beginning of Dissension....................111
Chapter VIII	–	Beginning of Reconciliation 132
Chapter IX	–	The End of a Beginning 158
Chapter X	–	Another New Beginning 181
Chapter XI	–	The Last Beginning 203
Postscript..214		
Maps 221		
Chronology 224		
Bibliography 226		
About the Author 228		
Index		230

Introduction

It is amazing that almost nothing has been written about William Edwin Hoy who surely must be numbered among the giants of the foreign missionary movement. He holds the rare distinction of having been a Christian pioneer in the two great countries of East Asia. For fifteen years he and his wife labored in Sendai in the Tohoku, then the hinterland of Japan, where he was co-founder of Tohoku Gakuin University and Miyagi Gakuin for Women, also starting a variety of other activities of Christian outreach. Then, when severe asthma forced him to seek a drier climate, he went to the interior of China where in Hunan, then hostile to foreigners, he soon founded two more schools, a hospital, and a work which became extensive throughout the province in his remaining twenty-seven years of service.

On the occasion of the 100th Anniversary of the founding of the two schools in Sendai, it is only fitting, and long since overdue, that proper justice be done to this towering figure. For without him, or someone like him, these two schools would not have been founded or have survived their early years. Thanks to his efforts, along with those of Oshikawa Masayoshi, at whose initiative the work of the Reformed Church in the U.S. was begun, these two schools bear the distinction of being pioneers of education in North Japan. Tohoku Gakuin is the oldest institution of higher education in Sendai, government schools included, and next to Toogijuku in Hirosaki, the oldest Christian school on Honshu north of Tokyo. Miyagi Gakuin is the oldest school for women both in Sendai and in the Tohoku. Hoy's career, however, became far more closely associated with the development of Tohoku Gakuin and with the evangelistic outreach of the church. This study focuses upon the Japan years because of the anniversary perspective which occasioned it.

If William Hoy had few peers, neither did his wife Mary, who came to Sendai as a single woman at the tender age of twenty-three to be one of the first two teachers of Miyagi Gakuin. Unfortunately, she left few writings, especially after her marriage, but it is clear that she and William were one in everything. As the record shows, William had no sympathy for what is now called sexism, and Mary combined creatively the three careers of housewife, mother, and missionary. In many ways they were pioneers, often a century ahead of their time. Yet they also belonged to that missionary era, which is now often dismissed with charges of religious intolerance and cultural imperialism. This is evident in Hoy's writings, but the context presents a somewhat different appraisal. No cosmetic attempts have been made. The record is presented as completely as possible, in the actual words of the participants. Hoy's candid writings reveal his flaws, especially his tendency toward self-righteousness and even paranoia. Yet in retrospect, his accomplishments are great, as is the indebtedness of all who have been his heirs.

The materials for this study are considerable, especially considering the destruction of war in Japan and China. Safe, of course, were the records of the Mission Board in the archives of the Theological Seminary in Lancaster, Pennsylvania. These contain Hoy's voluminous correspondence to the Board as well as the Proceedings of the

Japan Mission of the Reformed Church in the U.S. Another valuable resource is *The Reformed Church Messenger*, the weekly publication of that denomination, which printed regular reports and articles by the missionaries on the work in Japan. In recent years copies have been made of most of this material for the archives of Tohoku Gakuin University. Lost are the letters to Japan from the Board and all the Mission records in Sendai which were destroyed by the Ankeneys on Pearl Harbor Day. None of the Hoys' personal letters to their families remain, although their granddaughters, Dr. Camilla Hoy of Greensboro, North Carolina, and Mrs. Edle Waerum, of Namsos, Norway, supplied important data from family records and memory. It is regrettable that this research was not begun while the Hoys' eldest daughter, Gertrude, whom this writer knew well, was still alive. The Japanese materials, unfortunately, are few, partly because of the war, but mostly because the Japanese participants had no constituency to which they needed to report and also because they were not much given to recording such details. Most Japanese materials are official documents which contain data more fully treated in the Mission records, and therefore they have not been listed herein. This vacuum of information renders the record admittedly one-sided, with only hints concerning the perceptions of the Japanese.

The reader should note that the Japanese word order has been used for names of Japanese persons, with the family name first. Also, Chinese names are given in that old system of romanization used in Hoy's day which predates the current one. Then, the confusion between the almost similar names of the Reformed Church of the U.S., which was of German origin, and the Reformed Church in America, of Dutch origin, is avoided by referring to the former as the German Reformed church and to the latter as the Dutch Reformed Church. When only the term, Reformed Church, is used, it refers to the former, which is central to this study.

This writer is deeply indebted to Dr. Demura Akira, Professor of Church History, and Mr. Hino Satoshi of the Archives, both of Tohoku Gakuin University; to Mr. Watanabe Hiromichi and Miss Margaret Garner of Miyagi Gakuin for Women; to Miss Elizabeth Sanders of the Archives of Lancaster Seminary; to Mr. Lewis Dunn of Lancaster, and the above mentioned Hoy descendents. Above all, the author is grateful to Dr. Seino Tetsuo, President of Tohoku Gakuin University, and Dr. Kodama Shozo, Chairman of its Board of Trustees, whose friendship with the writer spans nearly four decades, for without their encouragement and support this volume would not exist.

Finally, this writer must confess that never has he done any research or writing which he has enjoyed as much. It has been a sounding of his own roots as well as a pilgrimage.

C.W.M.
Sendai
October 1984

Chapter I - BEGINNINGS IN PENNSYLVANIA

"I can give no more definite answer than that I grew up in Christ." Lancaster, Pa., October 24, 1884

Little is any longer known about the early life of William Edwin Hoy, but the most important thing there is to know is clear. He came from a family of rugged pioneer farmers who were devoutly Christian. He was born on June 4, 1858, just three years before the outbreak of the Civil War, in the old stone house built in 1818 by his grandfather, John Hoy, in the Buffalo Valley of the Allegheny Mountains about four miles from Mifflinburg in central Pennsylvania.

In the late 1700's John Hoy (1767-1849) had come from Berks County in eastern Pennsylvania, which by that time was already well settled, to join his uncle, Philip Hoy, who in 1773 had purchased a sizeable tract of virgin land in that new frontier. Tax records for 1775 show that Philip was assessed for ten acres of cleared land, some log buildings, two cows and two sheep. In 1796 John's name appears along with Philip's on the tax list. In 1803 Philip sold his nephew 149 acres of land and moved further west to Fairfield County in Ohio with several of his sons and their families. John had at least fifteen children by two wives, Barbara and Mary, and most of their names were from the Bible: Peter, David, Israel, Katherine, Abraham, William, Sara, Barbara, Lydia, Susan, Jonas, Elias, John, Mary, and Elizabeth. To enlarge his farm he kept clearing land and erecting sturdy buildings of stone, for he was also a highly skilled mason. He even constructed a "subscription school" with the neighboring children welcomed for a small fee. This three-storied building was near a stream with water running through a wooden trough into the ground floor near the fireplace. The classroom was on the second floor where the pupils sat on long benches made of split logs and wrote their lessons on pieces of slate which they held in one hand. On the third floor were the living quarters of the teacher and a sleeping room for the children when Indian trouble made it wise for them not to return home. When the first public school was started in 1847 at Turkey Run, a mile south, the school was used as a carpenter's shop for a cabinet maker, then as a farmers' equity store, and finally as a storage place. The stone and timber for the house and barn and school were all hand hewn, while the woodwork for the three-storied house was hand fitted with careful craftmanship.

The European origins of the Hoys are obscure and the explanations vary. One holds that John's father was named Albright and that he came from Scotland in the early 18th Century, citing in support of this British background the fact that Hoy is both a family and a place name in the Corkneys of northern Scotland. Another account gives John's father's name as Albrecht Heu and suggests a French Huguenot heritage. Yet another possibility is German which is consistent not only with the name but also with the immigration to the overwhelmingly German Berks County and with membership in the German Reformed Church. In any case the Hoys were pioneer settlers for whom their roots across the Atlantic were remote. In Union County, with its mix of Germans and British, they became staunch members of St. John's Reformed Church of Mifflinburg which was founded in 1806.

Jonas Hoy, William's father, was born on July 14, 1825, a twin of Elias. Their other brothers eventually moved to Ohio and one to Iowa, while all their sisters except Lydia married and moved away. The property had been divided to support two families, at which time John Hoy had built another house and barn at the other end of the farm. The twins and Lydia remained on the homestead. Jonas married Elizabeth Gebhart who bore six children, two of whom died as infants. On February 10, 1864, Elizabeth died at age 35 leaving her 39 year-old husband with four children ages 12 to 5. William was then 6. Jonas later married Catherine Brown who raised the children with the help of their beloved Aunt Lydia[1].

The family recollection concerning William's boyhood is that he always wanted to become a preacher. He would often take his siblings, Mary, James, and Ella to the ruins of the old cider press at the edge of the apple orchard of about 250 trees. There he would mount the old foundation stone hewn by his grandfather to preach to them and have them pray with him, and when he conducted a funeral he expected them to cry. Church records show that he was confirmed on January 24, 1874 by the Rev. George Addams. The Rite of Confirmation, conducted by those churches which practiced infant baptism, involved a period of intense instruction by the pastor in the catechism, which was a manual of questions and answers with biblical passages concerning the Christian faith and life. For the Reformed Church it was the Heidelberg Catechism of 1563. This weekly training, requiring at least several months, culminated in a special service in which the youths confirmed the baptismal vows made for them by their parents, confessed their personal faith in Jesus Christ, and promised to live accordingly. For a serious lad like William this must have been an awesome experience with life-long significance.

Sometime in the 1870's, Jonas and his sons remodeled and enlarged the old stone homestead entirely by hand. William, intent upon entering the ministry, proposed to his father, that instead of the inheritance he would someday receive, he be given the necessary theological education. Although this was not easy for his family financially, he went first to his denomination's Academy at Mercersburg for one year and then on to Lancaster for college and seminary. He was the first in his family to receive a higher education, and all were proud of him. Years later, in keeping with the agreement, when his father died he received nothing. One version of this story is that Jonas had included William in his will, but that William in Japan declined to accept anything, which was completely in accordance with his character.

In his writings William seldom referred to his family. His only mention of his mother is in an article in *The Messenger*, the weekly publication of the Reformed Church, written in 1887 a year after his arrival in Sendai, in which he described her peaceful death surrounded by family as an example of the Christian faith and motherhood much needed in Japan. "When," he asked, "will Japan rejoice in a Christian womanhood?"[2] Ten years later, when he learned of his father's death, he wrote to the secretary of the Mission Board,

> Distance now seems cruel. My father was for years a faithful

elder of the Mifflinburg Reformed Church. Well do I remember how he interested me in committing Bible verses to memory. He never once offered any objection to my becoming a foreign missionary, although it was a sore trial for him.

Although no other details of William's upbringing have been preserved, it is clear that his home was deeply Christian, faithful to the church, devoted to hard work, manual skills and the value of education.

William graduated from Franklin and Marshall College in 1882 and from the Theological Seminary three years later. Though separate institutions, the two were for all practical purposes the same. Seminary students lived in the college dormitory, classes were held in Old Main until the seminary building across the street was completed in 1894 and many of the functions of the two schools were held together. The college represented a merger in 1854 of Franklin College founded in 1787 in Lancaster and named after the famous American statesman, Benjamin Franklin, and Marshall College which had been formed in Mercersburg in 1836 and named after the fourth Supreme Court justice, John Marshall. The first president of the Board of Trustees of this newly constituted school was James Buchanan, later to become President of the United States, whose home was in Lancaster. This institution, which also had a three-year preparatory Academy, was devoted to the classical tradition of education within the Christian context. Its presidents were generally clergy as were many of the members of the faculty. The course of study was strictly prescribed, including Greek and Latin and the Classics, German, chemistry, biology, zoology, astronomy, anatomy, archeology, physics, philosophy, logic, aesthetics, psychology, geography, literature and religion. This curriculum had been established in reaction to the movement which was becoming popular under the leadership of President Eliot of Harvard which allowed students to elect their own courses. This purpose was clearly stated in the college catalogue.

> This college was created originally in the service of classical and liberal learning. It aims to be true to this object. We acknowledge the new type of study, but this experiment is not for Franklin and Marshall. Our college desires only those students who desire a full classical education for its own sake. It is interested in developing the whole personality and character of its students[4].

In addition to daily required chapel were a variety of religious activities such as prayer meetings and special lectures and programs. Discipline was strict, both morally and otherwise. No details about William's years there have been preserved, not even about the beginning of his friendship with his future colleague, David Schneder.

The records relating to Hoy's seminary years are all about his missionary calling[4]. An article in *The Messenger*, November 29, 1882 by Hoy, then in his first year, reported the Inter-Seminary Alliance Meeting on Foreign Missions in Chicago which he had just attended. Some 400 students representing 52 seminaries and 15 denominations of the U.S. and Canada attended along with several missionaries. Among the six students from Lancaster was David Schneder, then a senior, "who put his whole soul into his paper. His young person quivers as of intense earnestness." On his missionary application two years later Hoy cites this meeting as decisive for his calling. "Many of us heard the voice of God calling us to preach the Holy Gospel to every creature. I made up my mind to enter the foreign mission field." He also indicated that he had just returned from a similar convention in Princeton where 38 young men, himself included, had decided to seek missionary appointment. Upon returning to Lancaster he had seen in *The Messenger* the appeal for the third missionary of the Reformed Church which "sent a thrill through my whole being. I am ready to be sent to the uttermost parts of the earth. For me there can be no peace at home. If the Reformed Church can't send me, I'll seek a commission elsewhere."[5]

One question on the missionary application is worth examining along with Hoy's answer because both reveal much about the 19th Century missionary movement and the young candidate himself. The question, "When and where were you converted? Was it in a revival of religion?" reflects the Evangelicalism of that day which in its extreme form, known as Revivalism, had become one of the dominant themes of American Protestantism. This represented an expression of 18th century pietism which emphasized inner religious experience and salvation through personal conversion. This, however, was at variance with Reformation theology which emphasized Christian nurture through the Church from infant baptism through confirmation into a maturing Christian faith and life. In 1843 John Nevin, the famous theologian of Mercersburg, had attacked Revivalism as unchristian in his widely read and highly controversial, *The Anxious Bench*. The title referred to the special seat reserved for sinners who were about to confess their sins in public and be converted. For Nevin this represented the intrusion of an emotionalism which was short-lived and which produced little lasting fruit. Furthermore, while the conversion experience might be appropriate for persons who had grown up outside of the Church, or for those who had fallen away from Christ, it was hardly relevant to the faithful who had grown up in the Church. Yet, more importantly, such an approach was theologically unsound because it reduced salvation from a gift of divine grace to a human act.

This Evangelicalism, however, proved quite pervasive and even divisive in the Reformed Church. It became one of the issues in the Mercersburg Controversy which sapped much of the strength of that denomination for more than half a century, and which in turn was one of the chief reasons why the German Reformed Church was so retarded in its foreign mission outreach. Although its Board of Foreign Missions had been formed in 1838, its work, which was minimal, had been carried out through other well-established boards, namely that of the Congregationalists until 1866. It wasn't until the 1870's that preparations were made to open its own independent work. Japan was chosen as the field of endeavor in 1873, while the first missionaries, the Rev. Ambrose and Hattie Gring, were sent in 1879. The Rev. Jairus P. and Annie Moore followed four years later.

The Protestant missionary movement, from its inception at the end of the 18th Century, had been the child of Evangelicalism, beginning with the so-called Free Churches such as the Baptists and

Congregationalists, and spreading to the kindred spirits in other denominations. "The heathen world" presented a virgin field for Christian conversion and an unprecedented challenge for evangelistic activity. It was only natural that when the Reformed Church finally began its own foreign mission work, it would be strongly influenced by this prevailing ethos, even though such terms as "conversion" and "revival of religion" were alien to its tradition.

Hoy's forthright answer, "I can give no more definite answer than that I grew up in Christ," to the rather biased question skillfully avoided the issue by standing firmly within Reformed theology in which there was no dichotomy between nurture and commitment. The Reformed tradition was essentially evangelical. The first theologian of the Reformation to maintain that "the command to preach the Gospel to all nations binds the Church" had been Adrianus Saravia (1531-1611), a Reformed pastor in Antwerp and later Dean of Westminster. Like the older foreign mission boards of the Reformed family, such as the various Presbyterians and the Dutch Reformed, the newly emerging missionary outreach of the German Reformed Church was staunchly evangelical. The passion to promote commitment to the Christian faith along with personal piety encompassed Christian nurture through education as a concomitant of direct evangelistic proclamation. For such missionaries evangelicalism was inclusive of a variety of activities, especially education. This saved them from those less enlightened extremes of attitude and method which came to characterize certain other sectors of the foreign mission enterprise.

Hoy's appointment to Japan was at the board meeting on April 21,

1885, at Salem Church in Harrisburg. At the same meeting two "single ladies" were also appointed to begin a girls' school in Japan, Miss Lizzie Poorbaugh and Miss Mary Ault. The Board also endorsed the plan of the Sunday Schools to raise $5,000 to "erect a female seminary building in Japan," through gifts of $50 each[6]. This was in response to the repeated appeals from the Grings. An article entitled, "Shall we have an Educational Institution in Japan" in the June 20, 1883 *Messenger* had centered around a letter from Ambrose Gring from Tokyo. "We must have some place in which to educate the young of both sexes whom we hope to influence through the progress of our work... Such a school would tend, perhaps more than anything else, to establish our church here." Gring pointed to the fact that the Presbyterians, Methodists, Episcopalians, Congregationalists, Dutch Reformed all had schools for girls and boys. With the editorial comment that "The Reformed Church has always honored education as the handmaid of true religion," the readers were invited to send their gifts to Rudolph Kelker, the treasurer in Harrisburg. Hattie Gring was also strongly urging the Board to send out a single woman to start a "female seminary" which most of the other boards had already established. A long article written by Rev. T.S. Johnston, Secretary of the Foreign Mission Board, which appeared in the September 23 issue of *The Messenger* that year quoted the appeal from Mrs. Gring at great length. Her long letter was prefaced by a summary of the official actions of the board which endorsed the sending of a "lady missionary" and appealed to the churches to organize a Female Foreign Missionary Society to raise the necessary funds. It also indicated that three candidates had already applied, although no mention was made of starting a school for girls. This was about the time when the Moores arrived in Tokyo and they were not slow in adding their voices to this appeal, which finally was fulfilled with the appointment of Poorbaugh and Ault two years later.

Elizabeth H. Poorbaugh was born on December 27, 1854, in Berlin, Somerset County in western Pennsylvania. Her father, Josiah, was a merchant and an elder in the Reformed Church. Lizzie, as she called herself then, was a graduate of York High School and had taught at public schools during the winter and at Normal Schools in the summer. On her application to the mission board she made her acceptance dependent upon bringing along her little niece, Kittie, whom she had raised since infancy. Her answer to the question about conversion was simply, "I was brought up in the Church."[7]

Mary Ault came from pioneer families which had immigrated to Pennsylvania in the colonial period. Her father's family could be traced back three generations to Adam Ault, and her mother's, the Waggoners, four generations to her great-great grandfather, Jacob Waggoner, 1732-1808. Mary's father, John, (1836-1880) had been a chaplain in the Civil War and a pastor of the Reformed Church. Mary Belle was born on September 10, 1863, in Mechanicsburg near Harrisburg, the oldest of five surviving children, four of whom were girls. Her parents had died within a year of each other when she was only seventeen. In her letter of application to the Mission Board four years later when she was a senior at the Keystone State Normal School at Kutztown she wrote,

> Through the influence of my dear departed father, I, at an early age, expressed a desire to become a missionary. My parents always encouraged the desire which grew stronger as I grew older, and I now long to go. I feel the Lord has been opening the way for me. I am now an orphan without a home. My brother and sisters have good homes and are happy. I have nothing depending directly on me, nothing that could hinder my going to Japan. I am ready and willing, if it be the Will of my Heavenly Father, to give up all and devote the remaining days of my life in working for Him[8].

At that time her brother John was nineteen, her sisters Anna, seventeen, Clara, fourteen, and Blanche only twelve. On her formal application she stated that during the winter of 1882 she had taught school in Moselm, Berks County. "There was no church or Sunday School held in the place, so every Sunday afternoon I had the children assemble in the school room where we read a chapter or two of the Bible, had prayer, and sang several hymns." In answer to the question about conversion, she wrote, "When I was twelve years old, I was converted at my father's home in Littlestown. It was not in a revival of religion."[9] While "converted" was hardly an appropriate term for her, her simple answer reflected the degree to which her home had been influenced by Evangelicalism without falling into the extremes of Revivalism.

Hoy graduated from the Seminary in June 1885 and on October 15th was ordained into the Christian ministry and commissioned as a missionary at the General Meeting of the Reformed Church which was held at his home church in Mifflinburg from the 14th to the 19th. Articles of Agreement for Missionary Service were signed on October 26th by the Secretary of the Board, Dr. T.S. Johnston and the President of the Board, Dr. David Van Horne, and by Hoy. The term of service was "until providentially hindered or recalled by the Board." No mention was made of any furlough. The yearly salary was $700, with $50 annually for medical bills, $300 for outfit and freight, and $400 for transportation to Japan[10]. Such terms were both standard and minimal.

The departure of the three candidates, however, was indefinite because of the financial difficulties of the Board which was hardpressed in supporting the Grings and the Moores. Among the people of the churches, and even most pastors, there was little interest in foreign missions. To promote the cause, *The Messenger* carried articles in almost every issue by at least one of the four missionaries in Japan, along with reports from the Mission Board and pleas for support. It had been decided to send Hoy first, so that fall Mary took a teaching position in Mahonoy City, "not a very pretty place, with unpainted frame houses, dirt streets and plank side-walks."[11]

Later that fall the Board was able to send Hoy. Before leaving Pennsylvania he visited the Schneders in Marietta near Lancaster where David had been a pastor since graduating from the seminary two years previously. Schneder had been disappointed in not being chosen as the second missionary because he was single and lacked pastoral experience, which prerequisites were not applied to Hoy two years later. Furthermore, Hoy, unlike Schneder, had been able to obtain the required permission of his parents. But the Schneders were firmly dedicated to foreign missions, and Hoy in parting assured them that he expected to see them next in Japan[12]. Also accompanying Hoy were two Japanese students from Franklin and Marshall College, Kinzo Kaneko of Hanamaki, Iwate Prefecture in northern Japan, and another named Sato. Kaneko, from a well-to-do samurai family, had come from Japan the year before at the age of nineteen. He had entered the academy department at the recommendation of the Japanese consul in New York, who had been influenced by a student of the class of 1885, Yamanaka Masataka. Hoy had instructed Kaneko, who was known as George, in the English Bible, and under the influence of Professor E. V. Gerhart of the Seminary, Kaneko had been baptized on Good Friday 1885 at St. Stephen's College Church. About the other two pioneer students from Japan nothing is known[13].

The Seminary gave Hoy a warm farewell with a special service and a poem written especially for the occasion[14]. Hoy was its first graduate to become a missionary, for while Gring and Moore were graduates of Franklin and Marshall, Gring had gone to Yale Divinity School and Moore to Heidelberg Seminary in Ohio. Dr. Thomas Apple, Professor of Church History and much devoted to foreign missions, remarked in parting, "Well, Brother Hoy, I suppose that after you get out there you will start a college and a seminary." Hoy later wrote, "From that time forward, I determined to convert into actuality the idea which had entered my mind. On the way to Japan the question of mission schools was ever in my mind."[15]

Footnotes

1. Data received from Hoy family in files of Tohoku Gakuin archives.
2. *The Messenger*, Mar. 30, 1887.
3. Hoy letter to Board, Mar. 3, 1897.
4. Mensendiek, *A Man for his Times*, p. 11, f.
5. Hoy missionary application and accompanying letter, Oct. 28, 1884.
6. *The Messenger*, April 29, 1885.
7. Poorbaugh missionary application, Mar. 30, 1885.
8. Ault letter to Board, Jan. 15, 1885.
9. Ault missionary application, April 3, 1885.
10. Hoy Articles of Agreement, April 26, 1885.
11. Ault letter to Board, Oct. 1885.
12. Mensendiek, *A Man for his Times*, p. 22.
13. Franklin and Marshall College Obituary VI, p. 240–241.
14. *The Messenger*, Nov. 11, 1885.
15. H.K. Miller, *History of Japan Mission of Reformed Church*, p. 45.

Chapter II - BEGINNINGS IN JAPAN

"I already feel at home in this pleasant land. On the 14th of January I will move from Tokyo to Sendai. There I shall find a virgin field and a work that will engage all my powers." Tokio, December 26, 1885

When William Hoy arrived in Yokohama on December 1, 1885, the work of the German Reformed Church in Japan was only five-and-a-half-years-old and was confined to a few fledgling activities in Tokyo and environs. Denominations such as the Dutch Reformed and the Presbyterians had been in Japan for as long as two decades and their work was already well-established. Hoy and his four senior colleagues, the Grings and the Moores, represented the second missionary generation which, with the growing popularity of the West, faced unprecedented opportunities.

Christian work, however, was still in its infancy with missionary activity quite limited. Foreigners were largely confined to the treaty ports which meant that mission effort was mostly concentrated in those areas. Permission to live elsewhere was given only to foreigners under the employ of Japanese. Yet, as Western learning became popular, missionaries could rather easily become teachers outside the foreign concessions under the auspices of a Japanese guarantor. Also special permission was needed by foreigners to travel more than twenty-five miles beyond their places of residence which naturally limited missionary outreach. However, after the lifting of the ban against Christianity in 1873 due to political pressure from the West, permission was increasingly being granted for longer trips into the hinterland even for evangelistic purposes. Furthermore, foreigners could not buy or hold property outside the foreign concessions in the five treaty ports, although this restriction could be circumvented by the means of a Japanese proxy which most missionaries had little difficulty in arranging. Most importantly, with the gradual opening of the country to Western influence, interest in Christianity was increasing.

  The Grings, after living in a rented house in Yokohama during their first winter in Japan, had purchased a western house for $4,000 in Tsukiji, the foreign concession in Tokyo[1], where most of the missions of the various churches were concentrated. Gring had devoted himself for the first three years to what he called "preparatory work", namely, language study, compiling a dictionary, and translating the Heidelberg Catechism into Japanese. In 1881 he had procured a printing press and soon was publishing his own tracts for distribution[2]. He strongly recommended and defended this policy of carefully laying a foundation before commencing any direct missionary activity. In June of 1881 he had taken a three week trip with Japanese evangelists covering about 250 miles in northwestern Kanto to get experience[3], and a year later he rented a Japanese house in Tsukiji to hold religious meetings with the help of his language teacher who was a Presbyterian[4]. Later that year he "bought a little school for $90" which could accommodate two hundred pupils with quarters for a teacher at Motodaiku Cho near Nihonbashi to use for classes during the week and for Sunday School and worship on the sabbath. In the spring of 1884 the Motodaiku Church was organized as the first one of the Mission, which after its eventual relocation became known as the Kanda Church. To the Mission Board Gring wrote, "I am very happy in my work. There is no position in America, not excepting the presidency, for which I would exchange my work here."⁵

The Moores, unlike the Grings, had plunged into direct missionary activity almost immediately after their arrival in October 1883. In their rented western-style house in Tsukiji they taught some English while studying Japanese. With the help of their language teacher, Mr. Kitami, and their two servants, all of whom were Christians, they held Sunday services and other meetings. A year-and-a-half later they moved out of Tsukiji, which they held responsible for Annie's poor health because it was near Tokyo Bay. Through Mr. Kitami they made an agreement with a Mr. Fukushima, a Christian and the registrar at the Methodist Boys' School, who wanted to start his own school with Moore as the English teacher. With the help of Dr. Eastland, a dentist who was from Heidelberg Reformed Church in Philadelphia, they rented a Japanese house with a school room at 50 Kami Niboncho in one of the most desirable parts of Tokyo. With them came their Bible class from Tsukiji and half a dozen converts. In this new work the Moores were much aided by Yamanaka Masataka, who had recently returned from Lancaster where he had graduated from both Franklin and Marshall College and the Seminary. Their most illustrious convert was Nakajima Nobuyuki, then already becoming one of Japan's leading statesmen, whose introduction to the Christian faith was through his wife's friendship with Annie Moore. In 1887 when the Moores moved to the Tohoku this small congregation was merged with the house church of thirty members, gathered by the Eastlands who lived just across the street, to form the Bancho Church. This in turn became the Fujimi Cho Church, which under the famous Uemura Masahisa became Japan's largest and most prestigious church.

In addition to these ventures within Tokyo, whose population was then just a little more than one million, work was also begun in nearby Oji and several places in Saitama Prefecture by Japanese evangelists in cooperation with Gring and Moore. The first trip by Moore outside Tokyo was with Gring to baptize Yoshida Kanesaburo and his wife near the village of Koshigawa just up the river from Tokyo Bay. The Yoshidas became an outstanding Christian family. A son, Kikutaro, eventually graduated from the seminaries in Sendai and in Lancaster; the eldest daughter, Misao, was in the first class of the Girls' School in Sendai and then became Mrs. Hoy's assistant until she married a Presbyterian pastor; a brother of Kanesaburo was a pastor first in Japan and then in California, and a sister became a Bible woman in Tokyo[6].

Hoy had arrived in Japan without knowing where he would work. Tokyo was already "well-occupied," as the military jargon much used by foreign missions in that day put it. Accounts written much later indicate that there were two invitations, one from the south[7], identified as Kochi, and another from the North[8], but there is nothing in the primary sources to substantiate the former claim. Well-documented, however, is the fact that soon after Hoy's arrival the opportunity in the Tohoku (Northeast Japan) was dramatically presented by Oshikawa Masayoshi, an energetic evangelist whose activities were centered in

Sendai.

The paths that led the German Reformed Church to Sendai and the Tohoku were varied, and when they converged that day in the meeting between Hoy and Oshikawa everyone concerned was convinced that it was all according to Divine Providence. One path had been pioneered by the Grings, though the outcome was unexpected. In pressing the Board to send out a single woman and open a girls' school, they assumed that the site would be somewhere in Tokyo. Then after Poorbaugh and Ault were finally appointed, the problem was to find the best possible location for this new work. One late spring evening in 1885 when Hattie and their three small sons were sick in bed, Ambrose went out for a walk. At the Tokyo Union Seminary he happened to meet Dr. James Ballagh, the much-respected veteran of the Dutch Reformed Church who had been in Japan since 1861. In the course of their conversation Gring asked for advice about possible sites for the proposed school. Much to Gring's surprise Ballagh suggested Sendai.

Ballagh had just returned from an extensive evangelistic trip throughout the Tohoku. He had been much impressed with the opportunity in Sendai, and especially with the urgent request for a missionary from Oshikawa, who a decade earlier had been one of his students in Yokohama. He suggested to Gring that they go immediately to talk with Oshikawa who just happened then to be in Tokyo. Oshikawa urged Gring to accept the call himself, assuring him that certain prominent persons in Sendai would provide the necessary buildings and operating expenses for both a boys' and girls' school[9].

Gring demurred, but Ballagh had opened a second path that led to Sendai.

The third and more dramatic path was the one pioneered by Oshikawa. Born in Matsuyama about 1850, he was the fifth of seven children of the Hashimotos, a samurai family. At age eleven he had been adopted by the Oshikawas to become the husband of their daughter and their family heir. In 1866 he fought in an uprising aimed at the expulsion of the foreigners. Soon after his marriage two years later he was sent by his feudal lord with eight other young men to Tokyo to study Western learning at the small school which was a forerunner of Tokyo University. But when this venture was suspended in 1871 he moved to Yokohama to continue his study of English in the private classes of Dr. Samuel Brown of the Dutch Reformed Church, who was one of the first Protestant missionaries arriving in 1859. A year later he and eight other students were baptized by Dr. Ballagh, which marked the beginning of the famous "Yokohama Band," many of whose members became outstanding Christian leaders. This also represented the founding of the first Protestant church in the country. Oshikawa, therefore, was not only among the first dozen Protestants baptized in Japan but also a member of its first Protestant church. Although alienated from his father, he studied theology under Brown and Ballagh until 1876 when he went to Niigata to work with Dr. T.A. Palm, a medical missionary of the Scottish Presbyterian Church. He made the trip to that remote port city on the Japan Sea by foot through heavy snow, arriving on New Year's Day.

Oshikawa became a skilled evangelist, eager to spread the Gospel as widely as possible. In 1878 he was finally reconciled with his father so that his wife and infant son were able to join him. The following year he made a long evangelistic trip into the Tohoku with his coworker, Yoshida Kametaro, a native of Ishinomaki, north of Sendai. The two men were especially impressed with the opportunities in Sendai, and after the Great Fire of Niigata on August 7, 1880 destroyed their church, hospital and residences, they decided to relocate there because they considered that area more open to the Gospel than strongly Buddhist Niigata. During the previous decade Christian work had been started in Sendai and environs by a few Japanese evangelists and an occasional itinerant missionary. Three congregations had been organized, the Greek Orthodox in 1871, the Roman Catholic in 1878, and the American Baptist in 1880. Within six months Oshikawa and Yoshida had forty-five converts, and in May, the Sendai Church (Higashi Ichibancho Church) was organized with Yoshida as pastor. Oshikawa, who evangelized throughout the area, proved quite successful, so that by 1885 there were groups of Christians of the Reformed faith in such places as Iwanuma, Furukawa and Ishinomaki, as well as followers in other scattered places. In order to promote this growing work, Oshikawa determined to start a school for boys and one for girls in Sendai where education beyond the elementary level was limited to the Sendai Middle School. For this he needed missionary help, and so he turned to his revered teacher, Ballagh[10].

At first Oshikawa had hoped that the Grings would accept the challenge, but when they declined, he persisted, visiting Ballagh at least twice in 1885 with his appeal for a missionary of the Reformed fold. Since the other missions of Reformed background were already committed elsewhere, the best prospect for pioneering the Tohoku was the newly-arrived German Reformed group. There is no record whether Oshikawa knew about Hoy's appointment and impending arrival or whether Hoy and the Board knew about the invitation from Sendai. Apparently none of them did, for all the descriptions of that momentous day when Oshikawa and Hoy met at Ballagh's home just three days after Hoy's arrival portray it as a spontaneous event wrought by God alone. It is obvious that Hoy and Oshikawa were both caught up by what was happening and that each was much impressed by the other. Oshikawa, who was then thirty-five and in the prime of life, presented a most commanding figure. Noble and commanding in appearance, especially in kimono, full of energy and enthusiasm, possessed of many talents, resolute of will, able in speech, proficient in English, with ten years of experience in Christian work which had been crowned with much success, he surely had few peers among the Japanese Christians of his time. Much of the same was true of Hoy, then 28, different as he was in many ways. Though yet inexperienced, he was solid, determined, dedicated, tough, compassionate, a man of vision with the will and skill to turn dream into reality, the best type of foreign missionary of that day. Both Gring and Moore were also much taken by what was unfolding, and within a week Gring and Hoy were in Sendai with Oshikawa to look into this Macedonian call more closely.

    In those days before the railroad had been completed as far as Sendai, the trip was two days by coastal mail boat whose first class accommodations were considered quite comfortable by foreigners. From Mangoku near Ishinomaki a smaller boat provided service through Matsushima Bay to Shiogama, this scenic area comprising one of Japan's three traditional places of natural beauty. Then the trip in to Sendai by jinrickshaw took a couple of hours through the plain of rice fields. Sendai was then just a provincial town of about 60,000 and still completely traditional. Hoy was quick to report his findings to the Mission Board, and the Board in turn to the people in the churches through *The Messenger*.

Soon after my arrival in Japan the question of my future location was brought before me in a striking manner. It was this, "Should I go to Sendai or remain in Tokyo?" To answer it intelligently and definitely, Bro. Gring and I, with the hearty approval of Bro. Moore, went to Sendai last week and "spied out the land." What was the result of our examination?

Sendai is the heart of an important and hopeful section of country just feeling the influence of new life - the tremblings of beginnings, great in prophetic force and assurance; something that tells of the young manhood, strong, vigorous, courageous, that is born from within. This city, for the place it occupies in the present flow of progress and for its wonderful promise of becoming a great influence in the imperial government, is the center of the six millions of the seven northern kens. For the preservation of health and strength Sendai is certainly far preferable to Tokio.

The people of Sendai are still largely in their native simplicity. There are only five foreigners in the city. Just as you may see in the early stages of the day's dawn great promise of what is to be, so here in the faint light that is appearing one may find the confidence of the near future that is to make these people brighter and better. The Baptists and Methodists have recently opened evangelistic work here based on the educational system. A few years ago a Japanese evangelist began preaching Christ in this city and has now a congregation of one hundred and thirty members. The third day after my landing on these shores this native pastor asked me to come to his help. The Christians of Sendai are praying that the Lord send me to their place to preach the glad tidings. Those who do not embrace Christianity beg me to come. Christians and heathen ask for the bread of life. The citizens in general, backed by a few influential government officers, beseech me to make my home with them. They want foreign influence, education and example ; yes, thank God, they ask for the Gospel. Their desire is to have Christian agencies in their beautiful city. They would like to have a girls' seminary. There is no question but that Sendai is the most promising field, and the most urgent one in Japan for female education. The citizens beg that Miss Poorbaugh and Miss Ault be sent. If only our Reformed people at home could realize the intensity of this new purpose at work in the hearts of these people! It is a happy and holy privilege before God to love and help such a desire framed upon the lips of native Christians and echoed by the pleading voices of those still in spiritual darkness.

I am making arrangements to locate in Sendai. I could not otherwise. The call comes to me with a divine force that I cannot withstand. Property is cheap and good houses can be rented for four yen ($3.35) per month. I want to engage in teaching English, looking forward to the Bible and our Catechism. A boys' school may probably grow out of this. A number of bright boys are eagerly awaiting my return. One young Christian wishes me to direct his theological studies.

All the missionaries that I have thus far met are unanimous in the opinion that I can do the greatest good in Sendai. The voice of the Father calleth now even more forcibly than in that memorable moment of my life when I first publicly announced my consecration to the cause of foreign missions.

Sendai has become the heart of my hopes, and it will be, I trust, the hearth and home of my best missionary affections.

Yours in the Lord,
William Hoy

Endorsed by A.D. Gring and J.P. Moore[11]

The five foreigners, though not identified, were probably Father Protelande, a French Catholic priest who had arrived in 1878; Rev. and Mrs. Ephraim H. Jones, American Baptists, in 1884; and Dr. and Mrs. Herbert Schwartz, Methodists, in 1885. Although Schwartz was a physician, he was employed as an English teacher at the Sendai Middle School. There were also two cloistered French nuns who had arrived in 1882.

A basic problem in accepting Oshikawa's invitation was the fact that while the new work in the Sendai area was within the Reformed tradition, it was not related to any established church organization, and Gring had advised him that his Mission Board would not support any such independent activities. Furthermore, Gring and Moore had not formed any kind of organization for their own activities in Tokyo, resisting the formation of another church body in Japan because it meant transplanting American sectarianism for which they had no sympathy. Hoy had been sent, however, with the expectation of his Board officials that a Japan Classis of the Reformed Church in the U.S.

would be formed. But the missionaries preferred to affiliate with the Church of Christ in Japan, popularly known as the Union Church, which had been formed in 1878 by the American Presbyterian, the Scottish Presbyterian, and the Dutch Reformed (U.S.A.) churches. Since Oshikawa's background was with that group, a Tohoku Classis of the churches in the Sendai area was organized, joining the Union Church at its General Meeting in Tokyo in November 1885. Then on December 21, after Hoy and Gring returned from Sendai, the Japan Mission of the Reformed Church of the U.S. was officially organized, with Gring as president, Moore as treasurer, and Hoy as secretary. At its first meeting on January 1, 1886 the Mission voted to send Hoy to Sendai and to recommend to the Board the joining of the Union Church. The Board readily agreed, and on April 22 the new relationship became official. Both the missionaries and the board officials were committed to cooperation, and Japanese Christianity had been spared the anomoly of a German Reformed Church of the United States in Japan, not to mention Dutch and Scottish varieties[12].

Footnotes

1. *The Messenger*, April 14 and June 1, 1880.
2. *Ibid.*, May 18, 1881.
3. *Ibid.*, June 23, 1881.
4. *Ibid.*, June 18, 1881.
5. *Ibid.*, Jan. 1, 1883.
6. H.K. Miller, *History of Japan Mission*, pp. 44-67 and J.P. Moore, *Forty Years in Japan*, pp. 44-67.
7. Miller, *History*, p. 9.

8. *Tohoku Gakuin 75 Nenshi*, Hanawa, Ed., p. 64.
9. *The Messenger*, April 17, 1890 and *Mission Proceedings*, Feb. 2, 1889.
10. A.R. Bartholomew, *Won by Prayer*.
11. *The Messenger*, Jan 27, 1886.
12. Moore, *Forty Years*, pp. 68-76, Miller, *History*, pp. 8, 21, 45, 101-102, and C.W. Iglehart, *A Century of Protestant Christianity in Japan*, p. 55 f. and *The Messenger*, April 17, 1890.

Chapter III - BEGINNINGS IN SENDAI

"I cannot always wait at a distance of 8,000 miles for the long process of correspondence before entering upon certain lines of work. This is not hot enthusiasm running riot with my judgment." Sendai, Oct. 15, 1886.

Almost immediately after arriving in Sendai, Hoy settled down in a small rented Japanse house at 63 Kami Naka Cho near the Hirose River at Ohashi beneath the old castle site. In an article for *The Messenger* he poetically described in great detail his house and garden as well as the surrounding neighborhood. The house had two stories and was only two months old. The tiny gate from the street reminded him of the "needle's eye" in Jesus' parable, but in contrast to the biblical setting the main gate next to it was seldom used. He found his new home "so much like a large playhouse that one feels he has found a place where perpetual childhood abides, and the Japanese are childlike in many of their gentle manners."[1] He also had a servant, a Christian, "a living sermon to the Japanese. All his duties are performed to the minute. There has yet not been a single variation from scheduled time. His sense of decency, neatness and order go with his punctuality."[2]

The young missionary immediately threw himself into the study of the language under "an able Christian teacher," Saito Hidesaburo, who knew no English then, but who eventually became a distinguished linguist. Using the Bible as a textbook, before the end of the year Hoy was translating short Christian stories and sermons into Japanese as well as Buddhist sermons into English[3]. In another long article he described the intricacies of the language and his problems in learning it. "Do I like the Japanese language? Yes, decidedly yes! Why? Because back of this language is the beauty of the mind." He also indicated that his teacher would not let him use a manuscript when he began preaching, at the end of his first year[4].

The Messenger carried a continuous flow of articles by Hoy about his new abode, all skillfully written and full of warm appreciation. One praised the natural beauty of Sendai and the nearby mountains, the Izumi Gatake, from the panoramic perspective of the castle site. "I looked long upon the scene before me, but my eyes turned again and again to the place I call home. Home, thank God, I feel at home!"[5] In another he described the grave and temple of Sendai's first feudal lord, Date Masamune (1567-1636), concluding with a poignant expression of what this meant for himself as a missionary. "The fading beauties and departing glories of a magnificent worship are the shrouds of a dead religion, buried without a single ray of hope. I kneel upon a Christless grave and pour out my soul before the Throne of High Heaven for the City at the foot of these hills."[6] In yet another article, again on nature with a nightingale as his inspiration, he closed with the pathos of the human scene. "Here are three children approaching, clothed with sunlight only. They are covered with a crust of filth and sores, the imprint of generations of vice. The missionary goes up to them and gives them a few cakes which he happens to have in his pocket. They eat the cakes and smile."[7]

Such articles by Hoy, as well as those by the Grings and Moores, not only helped promote support of their work at home but also knowledge of a land and people about whom the vast majority of Americans knew little if anything. When multiplied by the many denominations at work not only in Japan but around the world, this represented a massive educational activity which was unique, in a time when, except for the churches, the world beyond the West was largely ignored. As a result the "mission minded" people in the churches became far more conversant and sympathetic with alien cultures than most other people. The basic purpose of such articles, of course, was not just to educate but to inspire support for the work and to confirm the excellency of what was Christian. Though a degree of paternalistic condescension was inevitable, the tone of most missionaries like Hoy and his colleagues was overwhelmingly appreciative and receptive. Where it was critical, as with the low estate of popular religion and many aspects of the human scene, this was not without reason. However, such missionaries were not given to condemning as sinful what was only different, or consigning to hell all who were not Christian. The "darkness" that pained them was not just dying without Christian hope but living without the Christian faith. Daily experience provided abundant examples of the differences in a day when the leaven of the liberal values imported from the West had still borne little fruit. The missionary passion was to make this life better in preparation for the perfect life to come. Salvation was not only in the future but for the present. That is why the missionaries engaged in a variety of activities, among which education was central.

    Hoy's invitation to come to Sendai was to engage in education, as was his permission from the government to locate there, which was arranged by Oshikawa. The best account of those beginnings is in Hoy's own words written a decade later to the Secretary of the Mission Board for an historical sketch of the work to date.

On January 13, 1886, I moved into my first Japanese home, a happy young man, conscious of having an important mission to fill in Sendai, and painfully aware of weakness and unfitness. Immediately a number of young men gathered about me, some for instruction in the Bible and others for the little English they might learn from me. For relaxation from the severe task of studying the Japanese language I taught these young men, some thirty, if I remember correctly, an hour a day. I soon came to see the opportunity of building up a good boys' school, and I began to write about the matter to our Board, but I received no encouragement. Dr. Johnston even rebuked me for writing too hopeful a letter on that subject. Brother Oshikawa and I met frequently to discuss the matter and to pray over it. Many a time did I arise at night to seek help and wisdom from God. One day Mr. Oshikawa came to my house and brought me the twelve pieces of silver, the story of which you know very well, and with tears in his eyes told me that our prayers were being answered. I shall never forget the simple joy and awful holiness of that hour.

I was told that there were six young men ready to come and be trained as preachers of the Gospel. The Spirit of God was upon me and I then and there solemnly promised Mr. Oshikawa to support those young men for one year. To meet these claims upon my meager purse, I had to devise the most rigid economy and the most systematic self-denial. I took God into partnership. I talked as freely with God as I may speak with you. He entered into all my projects. I thought and acted as if God were a member of my household, setting apart so much for God and so much for me. It was often my lot to go half hungry, to wear patched and insufficient clothing and to have to throw my clothing over my bed at night to keep warm. We met in a poor Japanese house in the most solitary part of Sendai and could afford no stove the first winter, having only a small charcoal fire to warm our fingers. With all these deprivations, however, this was the happiest school year of my life. We were all fully conscious that important and far reaching foundations were being laid, and we thanked God for the work of the present and the hope of the future[8].

The 'twelve pieces of silver', which have long since become legendary, were the gift of a Christian widow, Kami Chika. According to the legend, Mrs. Kami was poor and had saved the money for her funeral. At that time the coins, ichibugin, were no longer in use. They were evaluated by a bank as totalling only $4.50, so Hoy bought nine of them, which he sent to the Board suggesting they be sold to interested churchmen to raise a larger sum. Eight of them netted $25 and one is on display in the historical archives of Lancaster Theological Seminary[9]. According to a descendant of Mrs. Kami, who was recently located in Sendai, Chika was not poor, and the family legend has been that her gift was enough to live on for ten years. For Hoy and Oshikawa, more important than the money was the spirit of the gift and the inspiration it provided, so it became a cherished legend. The "poor Japanese house," which served as classroom and dormitory when the school was begun in June, was at Kimachi Kita Rokubancho, then at the edge of town. The teaching was done by Oshikawa, Hoy, and Sugata Yujiro, pastor of the Iwanuma Church. Known as The Sendai

1884

Theological Training School, its curriculum consisted of Catechism, Exegesis, Life of Christ, Fundamentals of Theology, Mental Philosophy, and English. In addition to teaching English, Hoy also taught other subjects through an interpreter. The seven students ranged from ages 19 to 32, one of whom, age 24, was married with three children[10].

From the very beginning Hoy urged the Board to support and expand his little school, and through *The Messenger* he appealed to the people in the churches. "A boys' school may grow out of this." Impatiently he urged the Board to accept the invitation from the people in Sendai to proceed with the two much desired schools. "The citizens beg that Misses Poorbaugh and Ault be sent soon."[11] But the policy of the Mission Board favored so-called direct evangelism. Gring and even Moore had devoted themselves largely to such outreach, although both were sympathetic to educational activity as supportive of evangelism. When Hoy was sent to Sendai the Board had "directed him to spend his labors primarily in evangelistic work, but that if favorable circumstances should seem to require it, the Board would approve his adding teaching to evangelistic labor."[12] Yet education had been the primary reason both for Hoy's invitation as well as for his permission to work in Sendai. More importantly, for Hoy evangelism and education could not be separated, either in policy or in practice. Education was the open door for evangelism, and evangelism required the training of a native Christian leadership. Gring wrote a twenty-five-page letter to Secretary Johnston urging the Board to seize the unprecedented opportunities in Sendai.

The government is beginning to see the benefit of their people mixing with foreigners. It is becoming more and more lenient and rather encourages than discourages foreigners, especially missionaries, to leave Tokio.... Older missions are already involved in places other than Sendai. This affords new opportunities to the smaller missions who have come to Tokio too late to compete with the older and larger missions. Tokio already has five large boys' schools... The Scottish Mission is fading because it has no schools to feed its work. It is a fact well understood that a mission that has no intellectual standing and literary influence is not of much importance in the eyes of this nation... Providence delayed us in Tokio so we could accept the challenge in Sendai... Hoy went to Sendai as cheerfully as a child to his home. If he had not come, we would have gone there. If we lose Sendai for a boys' school we lose it also for a girls' school. We must have four teachers by September, two for each school[13].

The problem with the Board, however, involved not only policy but finance. The pastors and the people of the Reformed Church were still slow in awakening to the challenge of foreign missions and funds were scarce. An article in *The Messenger* of April 28, 1886, stated that $12,000 was needed to support the existing work for that fiscal year and that out of the 1665 congregations with a membership of 174,000 about 1,000 had never given anything to foreign mission. To send the single "lady missionaries" a special appeal had to be made to the "ladies of the churches to elevate their sister women in Japan to the high standards of womanhood." The Board itself was a small operation of volunteers. Its secretary, Dr. T.S. Johnston, was a pastor in

Lebanon, while the treasurer, Rudolph Kelker, was a prominent judge in Harrisburg, about forty miles distant.

The opportunity in Sendai was made more urgent by the fact that the Congregational Board, which had been working in Japan since 1869, was negotiating with the officials in Sendai about opening a boys' school under the leadership of Rev. John H. DeForest, a veteran with twelve years experience in the Kansai. The initiative had come from Tomita Tetsunosuke, a native of Sendai, who had served as the Japanese Consul in New York before becoming the vice-president of the National Bank in Tokyo. Through his experience in America he had become interested in founding a school of western learning under Christian influence in his home town. He had also become much impressed with the Doshisha, the school founded by Niijima Jo in Kyoto in 1874. Niijima himself had been hoping for about two years to start such a school in Sendai. In May, just as Hoy was beginning his little school with the hope of support both from his Board and from Sendai, DeForest and Niijima arrived at the invitation of the Governor, Matsudaira Masanao, and a month later they returned to finalize the negotiations. Both DeForest and Niijima were quite sympathetic with the aspirations of Hoy and Oshikawa. The possibility of a union venture between the two denominations was considered but abandoned as too difficult. DeForest even offered to withdraw, but Hoy's board was not responding and the Sendai officials were intent upon procuring the more experienced and prestigious Congregationalists[14].

That spring the Mission Board had sufficient funds to proceed with the sending of the two single women. From Mahoney City, Mary Ault wrote to the Board Secretary for help in the preparations, adding the poignant comment, "I miss my father very much, whom I need for advice." She and Lizzie Poorbaugh were commissioned on June 1, 1886 at Salem Church in Harrisburg. Both gave short addresses about the need and challenges they faced. Mary recalled,

> Fifteen years ago my father took me, then a child of seven, to hear a lecture delivered by a missionary from India in the Bethel Church in Mechanicsburg. I do not remember much of what was said but well do I remember how loud the Lord called me, and on returning I told my parents I wanted to be a missionary. My dear father laid his hand on my head and said, "The Lord grant it, daughter." I seem to feel his touch and hear his voice yet.

On another note she said, "We are going amid an interesting and by no means ignorant people."[15]

The two women and Lizzie's six-year-old niece, Kitty, arrived in Tokyo on July 4th without knowing where they would be stationed, although it was understood that they would open a school for girls. This designation, therefore, marked an important development in board policy concerning educational activity. Moore wanted them to locate in Tokyo to help a Mr. Fukusawa start a school but Gring opposed this suggestion and Poorbaugh objected because Christianity was not to be included in the curriculum. It was soon decided to accept the invitation from Sendai because "the members of the Union Church seemingly one and all were so impressed with the urgent needs there." Among those strongly recommending this action was the esteemed Dr. Guido Verbeck, one of the first Protestant missionary to Japan. Before leaving Tokyo the women had hoped to visit some schools there, especially the Ferris Seminary founded by the Dutch Reformed Church in Yokohama in 1875, but the schools were closed because of cholera. There was, however, shopping to do for household necessities not available in Sendai. The September 29th issue of *The Messenger* carried a long article by Miss Poorbaugh about their days in Tokyo and their trip by sea to Oginohama where they were met by Hoy and Schwartz. They arrived in Sendai by rickshaw at 11 : 30 p.m. on "the second night of the Festival of Lanterns." They were met at the edge of town by a group of Christians with lanterns and the warm greeting, "We have waited so long for your coming." For all concerned it was a most propitious occasion. Lizzie wrote,

> The Christians of Sendai gave us our first formal welcome to Japan. About it all there was something solemn and awful in its suggestiveness. Coming into the land of our adoption so nearly at the hour when night and morning meet, we could not but hope that with our coming to Sendai might come to this people the dawn of a better, purer day, the day when the Sun of righteousness shall shine upon their benighted souls.

A small house at 35 Higashi Yobancho in the center of town had been provided by Sudo Rikuzo, one of those persons in Sendai who was interested in starting a school for girls. Preparations were begun to open the school in September, but this involved detailed negotiations with the prefectural office of the Ministry of Education by Oshikawa in cooperation with Sudo Rikuzo and Fujiu Kinroku, the latter being a member of the Yokohama Band who had been baptized by Ballagh. The school was officially registered as Miyagi Eiwa Jogakko, Miyagi English-Japanese School for Girls, with Poorbaugh as principal, and she and Ault as teachers. Control was vested in the teachers and the Board of Trustees, with Oshikawa, chairman, and Hoy, Moore, Sudo and Fujiu as the other members. Poorbaugh resisted making Oshikawa the head of the school and placing it completely under Japanese control, insisting that unless it was a mission school it would not have a Christian identity or purpose. She also was convinced that unless it was a foreign school it would forfeit much of the goodwill and interest of the people. She was quite surprised with the "punctilious requirements of the government officials" because she had "thought none of this would be necessary and that they could start small in their own house." She complied with every requirement except the one asking her to list the number of "native teachers" to be hired and the salary to be paid, replying that this would "depend upon the needs of the school as they developed."[16]

Classes were begun with six students on September 18th. The small house soon proved so inadequate that another was rented for classrooms at 51 Higashi Nibancho for ten yen a month. On October 15th Mary wrote to the Board that they had twenty-four students and "several more who speak of coming, but I'm afraid we will not be able to receive them because our rooms are about filled now. I came thinking there would be only a few private pupils at home, but the people want a good school which will cost considerable money." She informed the Board that two Japanese teachers were needed and that a Japanese house was not so suitable because it was dark, hard on the eyes, and couldn't be heated properly. The landlord would not permit stoves which required cutting holes in the walls, while the charcoal hibachi were inadequate and the fumes unhealthy. "But these things do not trouble us as much as the thought that we have to turn girls away. Our people at home are not yet awake to the needs of a heathen people." The governor and some of his friends had applied for the admission of their daughters, but "when they found that we would teach nothing more than Mrs. Jones does in her private class they preferred to continue with her." Therefore, Mary pleaded for $3,000 to build a proper school. "If we had a building all the pupils we have would be boarders." The teaching was in English and the students were both eager and able. Every Sunday afternoon she and Lizzie invited the girls to their home for an hour of Bible, hymns and prayers, with the help of an interpreter. She also asked for a book on calisthenics and some games like checkers to facilitate the language barrier. Of her first impressions she commented, "When we go walking we are always followed by a crowd of men and women and children. We felt very queer at first, but now we do not mind it so much." By Christmas the school had forty-one students including the daughter of the governor who himself was somewhat anti-Christian. Most of the students were daughters of physicians and military officials. That month the much needed teachers of Japanese and Chinese were employed in fulfillment of the government requirement[17].

In October the Congregationalists had opened the Toka Gakko

(Eastern Blossom School) with 120 boys. The name indicated the traditional intent of the school although its Christian orientation was implicit. Voluntary Bible classes were included in the curriculum but there were no chapel services. Five of the six Japanese teachers were Christian, the principal, Ichihara Morihiro, and two other teachers having been transferred from the Doshisha. Niijima was the honorary president. With DeForest and his family came another missionary, but in two months he was replaced by two new arrivals, the Rev. W. W. Curtis and the Rev. F.N. White. None of the trustees were Christian. The buildings, though inadequate, were provided by the Japanese along with the basic operating expenses in accordance with the agreement[18]. It was an auspicious beginning, marking the first venture of Christians in union with non-Christians in opening a school. In admiration Hoy wrote to Kelker, whom he always addressed as "Father," that the Congregationalists were the most successful of all the boards in educational work in Japan because "they educate young men and from among them raise up a native ministry." Then he pleaded for his own little school,

> A mission can do the most effective and abiding work only by educating a native ministry. He who trains 15 or 20 men for the ministry does infinitely more for the good of the cause than he who engages in preaching only. These boys will prove that this little school has not been in vain, though it was undertaken without the direction of the Board. I cannot always wait at a distance of 8,000 miles for the long process of correspondence before entering upon certain lines of work. Can't we establish a theological training

school in Sendai? This little school could be extended. This is not hot enthusiasm running riot with my judgment. We cannot depend on preaching alone!¹⁹

In another letter to Kelker concerning the rebuke he had received from Secretary Johnston of the Board, Hoy confided, "The unkindest cut I have ever received in my life is the information that some members of the Board regard me as a visionary and a dreamer... There are enough hardships here without the knowledge that men misinterpret my letters and endeavor to shirk responsibilities."²⁰ A special relationship of warmth and trust was developing between the young missionary and the senior official back home. Their exchange of letters was regular even after Kelker's retirement in 1890 and their correspondence helps fill in much of the hidden agenda of the more formal communications with the Board. Differences and misunderstandings between the Board and Hoy were not uncommon, and it was Father Kelker who became the interpreter and mediator.

While championing the cause of education, Hoy by no means neglected direct evangelism. During his first summer he informed the Board treasurer that he needed more than the $500 sent for such purposes, because "Tokio will need it all and there are calls from Furukawa, Fukushima, Yamagata, Yonezawa and Ishinomaki."²¹ That fall he asked for $100 to "open a new preaching place in Sendai and a number of Sunday Schools for little ones who run about the streets dirty and half naked. I want to put my theological boys to work. I cannot afford it myself as these young men need all my savings."[22] He also called for another missionary to come to help him. "I simply must have help. I can't stand alone. If you can't help me I'll have to call upon the Council of our Union Church."[23] The Moores had been requested to move to the new field in Sendai, but they had adamantly refused, even threatening to resign, because they insisted that their work in Tokyo should not be so abruptly terminated[24]. In November Hoy wrote about public lectures on Christianity in the Sendai Theatre with 1500 attending one evening session[25]. For *The Messenger* he described an evangelistic trip to Yamagata and Fukushima where the work was most promising[26]. Then on December 12th, just a year after arriving in Japan he preached his first sermon in Japanese and administered the Lord's supper to thirty-seven believers at the Iwanuma Church just south of Sendai.

> A little service in a strange tongue brings one nearer to the Father. But elation has not arisen. Difficulties of pronunciation and construction come in upon one constantly and keep him humble. I feel like a child climbing a steep mountain. Language is in its depth a life work. One year's toil is but a stepping stone before the temple of the foreign mind. To gain entrance into the Holy of Holies requires many years of training for the linguistic priesthood. The task of language makes the blood run young, and the life of words addeth flesh unto one's mental bones[27].

According to his first annual report, Hoy was conducting religious services in "a destitute section of Sendai and have already led a few souls to Jesus." He was also "teaching Sunday School to twenty-seven young men, four of whom had been baptized."[28] Of Oshikawa he wrote, "He is a man of good solid education and preaches with force and edification."[29] In summing up his first year he wrote to the Board Secretary that he loved his teaching and that the theological students were doing well. "This has been the fullest and richest year of my life. I could wish for nothing better."[30]

The opening of Toka Gakko had two important results for the budding educational activities of the Reformed Church Mission in Japan. It meant that at least initially the Girls' School would receive the priority in the development of general education by the Mission and that the endeavor for boys would be limited to theological training. When it soon became apparent that the promised support in Sendai of the Congregational undertaking would not be as much as had been expected, Hoy rightly guessed that the same would be true of the Girls' School, especially since the government was going to open the Dai Ni Koto Chugaku, the Second Higher College, for boys the following year.

> I do not see much hope of obtaining aid from the citizens of Sendai in procuring land and erecting buildings for a girls' school. The people are now raising $80,000 for a government school and they have not yet learned that it is worthwhile to help the women much. If they should assist us to a large extent, they would ask a corresponding control of matters. I pray our Reformed people might awake from their long missionary sleep and raise the means for a first class Female Seminary in Sendai[31].

In order to meet the needs of the growing school the Board issued a special appeal. In March 1887, with the gift of $1,100 from Rev. Dr. J.I. Swander and his wife of Fremont, Ohio, property was purchased for $1,400 at Higashi Sanbancho and Yanagi Machi Dori where the school remained until its removal to Sakuragaoka in the suburbs in 1980[32]. Because the transfer of funds via London was time-consuming, the down payment of ¥140 was advanced by the three missionaries in Sendai, Hoy, Poorbaugh and Ault[33]. The large lot had three thatched roof houses "not at all adapted to the wants of foreigners." The Girls' School moved into the two better houses and the other provided a more convenient and economic location for the Theological Training School[34]. Lizzie, Kittie and Mary continued to live at Yonbancho not far away.

In just one year the new Christian beginnings in Sendai, though modest, were many, and with the opportunities they presented came new imperatives.

Footnotes

1. *The Messenger*, March 31, 1886.
2. Hoy letter to Kelker, Feb. 8, 1886.
3. Annual Report of Hoy, Jan. 24, 1887.
4. *The Messenger*, Oct. 6, 1886.
5. *Ibid.*, May 26, 1886.
6. *Ibid.*, June 2, 1886.
7. *Ibid.*, July 14, 1886.
8. S.N. Callender, *Historical Sketch of the Work of Foreign Missions*, p. 23.

9. *The Messenger*, July 28, 1886 and *Mission Proceedings*, Feb. 2, 1889.
10. Hoy letter to Board, Dec. 15 1886 and July 1, 1887.
11. *The Messenger*, Jan. 27, 1886.
12. Callender, *Historical Sketch*, p. 21.
13. The Messenger, Mar. 3, 1886.
14. C.B. DeForest, *Evolution of a Missionary*, p. 147 f.
15. Ault Letter to Beard, April 1886, *The Messenger*, June 9, 1886.
16. Poorbaugh letter to Board, July 29, Aug. 21, Sept. 28, 1886.
17. Ault letter to Board. Jan. 5, 1887.
18. C.B. DeForest, *Evolution of a Missionary*, p. 155f.
19. Hoy letter to Kelker, Oct. 15, 1886.
20. *Ibid.*, Oct. 10, 1886.
21. *Ibid.*, July 14, 1886.
22. *Ibid.*, Oct. 17, 1886.
23. *The Messenger*, Nov. 6, 1886.
24. J.P. Moore, *Forty Years in Japan*, p. 73f.
25. Hoy letter to Kelker, Nov. 6, 1886.
26. *The Messenger*, Dec. 1, 1886.
27. Hoy letter to Kelker, Dec. 14, 1886.
28. Hoy Annual Report, Jan. 24, 1887.
29. Hoy letter to Kelker, Nov. 3, 1886.
30. Hoy letter to Board, Nov. 16, 1886.
31. Hoy letter to Kelker, Feb. 5, 1887.
32. H.K. Miller, *A History of the Japan Mission*, p. 111.
33. Hoy letter to Board, Mar. 30, 1887.
34. Callender, *An Historical Sketch.*, p. 36.

Chapter IV-BEGINNING IMPERATIVES

"O send us help ! You can if you will !"
Sendai, Nov. 13, 1887

At its first meeting in Sendai on September 29, 1886, the Japan Mission had urged the Board to begin an "English Biblical Training School" with the assurance that "it will not interfere with the evangelistic work." Hoy kept imploring the Board to support and expand his little training school for that purpose. "It is already doing a good and encouraging work, but it is evident that I can't forever support it entirely alone." At its January 28, 1887 meeting the Mission recommended that the Board concentrate its work in Sendai and support the Training School.[1] The Board concurred, and with the appiontment of Schneder that summer, the expansion of the school was assured. Along with its commitment to the Girls' School this represented a change in Board policy. A decade later, Board Secretary Callender acknowledged in his historical sketch of the Japan Mission that "the policy of supplementing evangelistic with educational work by establishing Christian schools, which has become so characteristic of the Board's work, was brought about largely by the untiring labors and self-sacrificing persistence of William Hoy."[2]

As the work in Sendai entered its second year, it was agreed that priority should be given to the erection of a proper building for the Girls' School, estimated to cost from $8,000 to $10,000.[3] "Let not want of money retard a work which is already doing much for the girls and women of Sendai."[4] For *The Messenger* Hoy described the closing exercises of the first year.

> When I saw the small rooms into which teachers, pupils, and visitors crowded, I grew honestly indignant at the thought that perhaps the ladies will have to teach another year in buildings of this kind. Let it not be so! Misses Poorbaugh and Ault have done a work of which you can all speak praises. Send your best praises in Gold to Hon. R.F. Kelker.[5]

He also informed his readers that the Japanese Minister of Education had told him that "if we in any way meet the wants of female education in Sendai, the government will not establish a girls' school, but if we do not, they will open one next year". This led Hoy to chide General Synod back home for allotting only $15,000 for the next three years for foreign missions and to challenge the Board to start a movement in the churches to raise the money needed for the desired buildings.[6]

A more graphic description of the primitive facilities of the Girls' School was given by its principal.

> As to the personal comfort of the girls or teachers in the house we now occupy I cannot pretend to consider at all. When we gather into the school room in the morning every available inch of sitting room is occupied. When the first class is called, the girls occupying the recitation bench go out on the veranda and let the class have their place and when the class is seated the first girls crowd back into the class desk seats. Miss Ault and myself sit on little bench-like chairs which always reminds me of sitting on a pantry shelf to which one

must hold tightly to keep from falling off. I've sent to Tokio for two little basket chairs but doubt whether we can find room for them.

Poorbaugh also mentioned the opposition of the Governor against "our determined practice of inculcating Christian doctrines". Threats had been made to take the girls away from school. "This was the second time the high authorities tried to discountenance our work, but both times the objections were overcome".[7] In another letter she described the simple house in which the three of them were living.

> In our house we are as comfortable I suppose as one can be in a Japanese house in winter. In our sitting room we have removed the paper covered sliding doors that stand between us and the elements, and have put in glass instead so that we do not live in darkness. But owing to the heat of the stove having warped the frame work everywhere the house is much more airy than is comfortable and I find it almost impossible to keep warm.

Lizzie concluded by praising Hoy whom earlier she had called a "born missionary".

> I must congratulate you for selecting Mr. Hoy as a missionary to Japan. Of course, I know you know and appreciate his worth, but seeing his earnest devotion to his Master from day to day and his especially earnest endeavors to carry out the instructions of the Board, his indefatigable, labors though in great discomfort from a local affliction, I could not refrain from expressing this estimate of our young brother who is every day gaining greater hold on the hearts and confidence of the people.[8]

In addition to her many duties Lizzie also educated her young niece with the help of other missionaries. Kittie was a happy, healthy child, and when the four DeForest children moved to Sendai three months after her own arrival she had a playmate, Charlotte, who eventually became the president of Kobe College for Women. Kittie was quite an attraction in Sendai and often mentioned in the letters of her aunt to the Board Treasurer, whom Lizzie, like Mary, also addressed as Father Kelker. This kindly old man, so devoted to missions, sent Kittie presents for her birthday and at Christmas, and she wrote him letters of which about a dozen have been preserved. One written about a year after her arrival, when she was seven, is worth including.

Thanks for the beautiful "Pilgrims Progress". It is such fun to read the book. Aunt Lizzie reads to me in the afternoon and evening when I am in bed. I do not like Japan a bit. They never comfort the babies a bit when they cry, and the poor things seem as if they never go home to their mamas, or ever get fed. It nearly breaks my heart to see the poor little babies so badly taken care of. Three days I go down to Mrs. White's to recite reading and physiology lessons and music, and three times a week Miss Ault teaches us drawing. Aunt Lizzie teaches me geography and arithmetic. Mrs. Moore gave me a little dog. He is black and white and his name in Rollo. I am just as happy as happy can be with my doggie. I like him even better than my dolls because he is alive.

Your loving Kittie.[9]

Mary led a busy life. She taught in English five mornings a week from 8 : 30 to 12 : 30 and used her language teacher as an interpreter when she taught the Bible. "The little girls learn so rapidly and when I tell them a Bible story listen so attentively. I love the people of Sendai. They are gentle and pleasant to work among. I thank the Lord for calling me to such a glorious work."[10] In the afternoon from 2 to 4 she studied Japanese. She also taught music to the boys in the training school. Within a year she was teaching Sunday School in Japanese, though she confided to Kelker that it took her a whole week to prepare the lesson. About the situation in general she commented,

> There is a perfect rage for English in Japan at present. Old and young want to study. It gives the missionaries a very good chance to meet all classes of people, though I must say I did not like the idea of teaching so much English and so little Bible. I see now that if we can be a little patient we will have plenty of Bible work before long.[11]

During his second year in Sendai Hoy became increasingly concerned with the problem of missionary housing. Almost from the beginning he had had problems with his health which he attributed to living in a Japanese house. His first summer he had had "a touch of malaria" which he blamed on the proximity of his house to the river. In November he had moved to 16 Minami Machi Dori on higher ground in the center of town. His letters become dotted with references to his poor health and the inadequacies of Japanese houses along with pleas for western style residences both for the women and for himself. In his appeal for the much-needed building for the Girls' School early in

1887 he included two western style houses at the cost of $2,500 each, insisting that "there is no economy in making missionaries live too long in Japanese houses."[12]

Hoy's concern for proper housing was not just due to considerations of health, as important as they were. Western style residences were far more suited for various missionary activities, not to mention more comfortable daily living. A year after his arrival he wrote to his confidant in Harrisburg that it was "not good not to be married", and that "bachelorhood is a hindrance to my work." Two foreigners before him had led "vile lives and left illegitimate off-spring. Shall I remain single? It is a fearful strain on a man's mind to be alone and to have no one to talk to." Roman Catholic celibates "lose much of their intellectual energy". He asked if there would be any objection if he married within a year or any difficulties over salary. He closed by saying he had "no right to use the name of any lady. I have not yet gone through the conventional preliminaries".[13] On July 20, 1887 he and Mary Ault were engaged. A month later Mary wrote to Kelker,

> By this time you have received Mr. Hoy's letter telling of our engagement. The Lord has blessed me far more than I deserve. I feel that I am scarcely worthy of so good a man. Mr. Hoy is a fine Christian gentleman and a model missionary. He is so good, so kind and gentle and loves me so much. I am very, very happy.
>
> When I came to Japan I gave myself up to the Lord and said if it was His Will I would spend my days in the Girls' School. He has seen fit to change the order of work. It is not without a feeling of deep regret that I give up my position as teacher in the school. Yet

I sincerely hope my getting married will not stop my working. There is a great work to do among the women of Japan. So while Miss Poorbaugh is teaching the daughters I hope to work among the mothers.[14]

Lizzie's comments to Kelker are also worth recording.

Mr. Hoy is too valuable a missionary for us to let him run the risks of living uncared for. I do not think it is climatization or the study of Japanese that breaks missionaries down so much as the terrible strain and loneliness from which we all suffer, and Mr. Hoy has felt it intensely. As for Mary, I greatly rejoice that she has won the love of a man as worthy of her, and in marrying Mr. Hoy she need not give up her purpose of being a missionary. It is surprising to me everyday to see the amount of mission work done in Sendai by the married women with growing families. So while I am very sorry to lose her in the school, I heartily rejoice and sympathize with them in their new-found happiness.[15]

The work in Sendai was much strengthened by the closing of the work in Tokyo beginning in 1887. With the expansion of the activities in the Tohoku it had become increasingly evident that the Board lacked the resources to maintain two centers and that the "largely unoccupied field in the North" was more challenging. Tokyo was already "well occupied" by many more established missions and the various activities of the Grings and Moores could easily be handed over to the Union Church. Furthermore, if the German Reformed Church did not respond adequately to the opportunities in the Sendai area, that field would be assigned to some other denomination in accordance with the agreement for co-operation among missions known as comity. Hoy strongly urged the Board to concentrate upon the virgin field in the Tohoku. "A mission as small as ours cannot maintain two centers of work. One or the other must go down, or both suffer injury. As we are in the Union there is really no loss in the cause of Christ in case we give up Tokio. This is the sentiment of the Mission."[14] Moore, however, urged the necessity of keeping a base in Tokyo, while Gring was undecided, his position changing with time and place.[17]

The Grings were not in good health, and as early as March 1886 the Mission had recommended a furlough for them, which the Board finally granted a year later.[18] That May they returned to Pennsylvania where Gring became increasingly critical of Board policy and practice. A month earlier the Moores moved to Sendai after it was finally decided to withdraw from the work in Tokyo and turn it over to the Union Church. Their refusal to do so the year before had not been because they shied away from the rigors involved, which both Secretary Johnston and even Hoy had assumed. Nor was it because of Annie's health which was generally uncertain and sometimes quite poor. Their acceptance of the hardship post in Yamagata that summer refuted such suspicions. Rather it was because both of the Moores had felt that their work in Tokyo could not at that time be turned over to others.[19] They travelled to Sendai in the horse-drawn wagon they had brought from Pennsylvania which had been much admired in Tokyo. Then in August they accepted the repeated call from Yamagata to help start an English-Japanese school there. They crossed the Sekiyama

Pass on a road so narrow that the wagon and its contents had to be carried by coolies at several places. In remote Yamagata the piano they had brought with them from America was such a curiosity that Annie charged one *rin* to see it and another *rin* to hear it, using the proceeds for their work.[20] This income surely was not much, for the *rin* was the smallest coin.

In the Sendai area evangelistic and church work were progressing well. At the end of Hoy's first year he reported that 92 members had been added to the three churches related to the Union in just one month. The following May he informed the readers of *The Messenger* that 2,550 converts had been won in just six months, commenting that while "the first converts in Japan had cost $60,000 each, a few years ago the rate was $400, and now in the last six months in and around Sendai it is $2."[21] That year the Miyagi Classis of the Union Church was organized, with the Mission contributing three yen for every one yen by the Japanese, while the committee was half missionary and half Japanese.[22] Hoy was enthusiastic over what was happening.

> I daily thank God for having brought me to this land. in which I may be of the least service in His Kingdom. Humble as my gifts are, I can nevertheless do much more here for his glory than I possibly could in America. My mind is at peace and my heart full of joy at the thought of serving God all my life in the capacity of a foreign missionary. Here is my work and here is my home.[23]

But he was overworked, had troubles with his health, and was constantly pleading for more help. With the delay in sending the Schneders he became impatient. In September after the Moores moved to Yamagata he cabled the Board to send the Schneders immediately. Two months later he wrote the Board, "Did you send me here for this? There's too much work in Sendai for one man. When will you send us Brother Schneder? O send us help! You can if you will."[24]

Hoy's health had deteriorated so much that he became somewhat desperate. In a long letter addressed to "Dear Reformed Friends," which was published in the November 23rd issue of *The Messenger*, he cited the example of a "heathen shrine in Tokyo" which raised $70,000 in contrast to the Reformed Church which had as yet raised only a few thousand dollars for the Girls' School building. "Don't you see the heathen are in advance of you? Do they love their gods more than you do Christ?" He concluded by revealing the fact that for the past five weeks he had been suffering from a disease which threatened to become chronic and that his physician traced the source to the fact that he was living in a Japanese house. "These houses can never be adapted to the wants and needs of Americans or Europeans".[25] A few days later he wrote to Allen Bartholomew, the new Board Secretary, in such a shaky hand that his weakened condition is obvious. After stating that he was going to Tokyo for a general evangelistic meeting at which time he would also seek further medical advice, he poured out his heart,

I cannot bear the thought that this bodily trouble is brought on by the negligence of our dear Church. I love the Reformed Church, but if she in her indolent missionary spirit in not providing proper accommodations for her missionaries causes me to become a physical wreck, she may have to pay dearly. I have sacrificed enough. The Reformed Church can't ask more unless she expects me to die. I am not ashamed nor afraid to say that our Board does not exercise enough faith in the Lord Jesus Christ. Their slow actions are just what the devil asks for and laughs at.... Talk, Talk! School boy talk! If I break down finally in health the Church shall know the reason. I have warned the Board but they have not listened.[26]

From Tokyo he wrote, "I dread the exposure of another winter in a Japanese house. Pray that the Lord may bless the physician's work so that I may be perfectly restored to health."[27]

Back in Sendai Hoy was not long in apologizing for the "critical letters" he had written while sick. To Kelker he wrote, "I should have been in bed. My head fell down upon my desk repeatedly, and by a tremendous effort of the will I sat up again and wrote a few sentences."[28] With Bartholomew he pleaded that his weakened condition had been aggravated by strong medicine. "Sick men sometimes say or do things that they would not think of in times of good health. If I wrote anything unjust or unkind, please forgive me."[29] Before the end of November he had moved into another house nearby in Katahira Cho, but soon he became so weak that Mary came daily to take care of him. When his physician, Dr. Schwartz, advised that he should stop working, he promptly wrote a long letter to the Board. "O this is hard to do. God has ripened a glorious harvest all around us. Must I be idle ?" About a disturbing report that had just reached him privately, he wrote,

> My dear Brother, it is all very nice to have a body of men sit in judgment on us and call us "fully consecrated" and express "deepest sympathy" with us in our work and trials, but the poetical vanishes, like the many hues of a day dream, when one learns that the same body of gentlemen in earnest conclave sitting, talk about missionaries not needing the house comforts of respectable American citizens. Let the Japanese speak for our consecration to our work. We are not ashamed before man or God to ask for houses suited to our life and work. In the name of God and in the love of souls I pray that no misguided conception of missionary economy will lead our Board to sin unjustly and inhumanly against our mortal bodies. Even the apprehensions of our dear Japanese brethren are decidedly on our side. Dear Brother, hear me, I am not angry. It is only a deep rooted love of souls asking for a strong body to live in and a good place to give it new strength. Common sense permits me to believe that the Board has not fully realized yet what other Boards had to learn by sad experience and what I am now exemplifying in my shattered health.[30]

Hoy became so sick that at his own request Dr. Schwartz moved in with him "to nurse and dose him." In a long letter to Kelker the doctor described the inadequacies of Japanese houses and strongly recommended that his patient be provided with a proper western house.[31] Lizzie advised Kelker that "Hoy seemed insane at times, but of course we knew it was the effect of being injudiciously treated by his physician, and that only added to our anxiety. Our Tokio physician says our breakdowns come from the houses we live in."[32]

William and Mary had planned their wedding to coincide with the arrival of the Schneders in Yokohama on December 21st because the presence of the U.S. Consul at the ceremony was necessary. But due to William's illness the wedding had to be postponed. Lizzie and Kittie went to meet the Schneders and two school girls came to stay with Mary so she wouldn't be alone. But after the first night Mary decided this was not necessary. The next night a robber tried to get in, but the cook heard him and chased him away. To Kelker Mary wrote, "I do not feel a bit brave this evening. It was wrong to be such a coward, but when robbers are around I become sort of panic stricken and do not trust in the Lord as much as I should."[33] Then William improved enough to go to meet the Schneders, and the wedding took place on December 27th in Tsukiji at the home of Mrs. E.R. Miller of the Dutch Reformed Church. Mrs. Miller had been the first single Protestant missionary woman in Japan (Mary Kidder, 1869) and she had founded the first Christian School for girls in Japan, the Ferris Seminary. The ceremony was performed by Moore who had come from Yamagata without his wife who was not well, with Schneder assisting, in the presence of many guests including both Poorbaughs. The honeymoon was at Atami, a hot spring on the seashore near Mt. Fuji. The Kelkers sent table linen, about which Mary wrote in thanks, "We have been invited out to some very big dinners given by the highest officers in Sendai and the table linen was the poorest muslin."[34]

By the end of 1887 the Sendai Church had a membership of about

400. In December alone there was an increase of 70. One Sunday seven soldiers were baptized.[35] That fall after several months of negotiations Oshikawa had arranged for the Sendai Church to purchase an old unused Buddhist temple of the Pure Land Sect at Minami Machi Dori and Nibancho. It was an excellent central location almost adjacent to Hoy's rented house and not far from the Girls' School or the "ladies home." The property had been taken over in default by a bank, and despite the opposition of its former owners it was finally sold to the church for $2,300. With the pending opening of the railroad, the price had gone up during the negotiations, and at the last moment one buyer had even offered $3,000. The old temple building was used not only by the congregation but by the Training School as its third location in just one-year-and-a-half. For Hoy this meant "rescuing a building from the gross use of idolatry and turning a heathen temple into a House of God."[36]

The railroad to Sendai was opened on October 15th with the Meiji Emperor on the inaugural run. This not only facilitated the Hoy wedding and the arrival of the Schneders but also missionary outreach in general, not to mention the many other changes that it brought. In January the Hoys began going to Shiroishi about forty kilometers south of Sendai. On their first trip, accompanied by their language teacher, Hashimoto, they visited a school of 700, as well as a hospital where they passed out tracts. They found so much interest that they decided to go regularly to hold classes.[37] Three weeks later they were befriended by the Koyamas who gave them the second floor of their house for their meetings. Dr. Koyama, a physician, had become a

Christian under the influence of Oshikawa six years previously. Forty women attended Mrs. Hoy's meeting in which she used Bible portions printed on "our mission press." Some New Testaments were sold. Mrs. Hoy also taught some girls to knit. One girl asked her to knit a "bag for idols," which she did. The Hoys were happily surprised that even their rail fare was paid.[38] In the same letter Hoy also described a visit by Schneder and himself to Hobara to baptize the first twenty-three converts there. The service lasted from 6 : 30 p.m. to midnight because there were three sermons, one of which was by Hoy. They were treated to a sukiyaki party whose gaiety reminded Hoy of "the Franklin and Marshall laugh, that innocent smiling aloud."

As Hoy entered his third year of missionary service he was highly optimistic about the situation. "The Japanese desire spiritual bread. The very progress of Japan is witness to the effort to rise above nature. Humanity moves onward and upward, and this nation is in this movement too."[39] He was also encouraged with the development of the Union Church, especially when the Congregational Churches, whose educational policy he so admired, joined in the spring of 1888. "This will set the great soul power to work with almost military precision. March! Victory!"[40] Together with his colleagues he was firmly committed to missionary cooperation and Christian unity. On the mission field this had become for him an imperative. "For myself, I have no longer any denominational feelings. One has no room for it here. The Japanese Church may yet teach all the nations the commentary on John 17." (Jesus prayer that all his followers be one.)[41]

After her marriage Mary continued teaching at the Girls' School until her replacement, Emma Poorbaugh, Lizzie's sister, arrived that summer. This increased the number of missionaries of the Reformed Church in Sendai to six, with the other two, the Moores, in isolated Yamagata. Sendai had become the center of the Japan Mission of the German Reformed Church. A good beginning had been made, and much of the credit belonged to Hoy. Two schools were established and under Board support. New evangelistic activities had been begun. The various locations of the Mission in Sendai were within a few minutes by foot from each other, the Girls' School at Sanbancho and the Poorbaughs at Yobancho, the Theological Training School and Sendai Church at Nibancho with the Schneders nearby, and the Hoys at Katahiracho not far away.

The challenge now was to develop what the pioneers had begun. The tasks were gigantic and the workers few, with the needs always exceeding the funds. The missionaries numbered only five and all were young. Poorbaugh at 33 was the oldest, with Schneder 30 and Hoy 29, while Mary Hoy was 24 and Anna Schneder was only 20. Their senior in every way was Oshikawa at age 38, for with their limitation of language and experience in Japan, they could have accomplished little without him and those Japanese devoted to the work. It was all a joint venture across the many barriers of the Pacific, with each side mutually dependent upon the other.

Footnotes

1. *The Messenger*, Jan. 16, 1887. Mission Proceedings, July 29, 1886, Jan. 28, 1887.
2. Callender, *An Historical Sketch*, p. 19.
3. Hoy letter to Kelker, Mar. 30, 1887.
4. *Ibid.*, Feb. 15, 1887.
5. *The Messenger*, July 1, 1887.
6. *Ibid.*, Sept. 12, 1887.
7. Poorbaugh letter to Board, Sept. 7, 1887.
8. *Ibid.*, Feb. 1887.
9. Kittie letter to Kelker, June 15, 1887.
10. Ault letter to Kelker, Jan. 28, 1887.
11. *Ibid*, Aug. 24, 1887.
12. Hoy letter to Board, Mar. 5, 1887.
13. Hoy letter to Kelker, Jan. 15, 1887.
14. Ault letter to Kelker, Aug. 24, 1887.
15. Poorbaugh letter to Kelker, July 24, 1887.
16. Hoy letter to Kelker, Nov. 5, 1887.
17. Moore, *Forty Years*, p. 73f.
18. Japan Mission Proceedings, Mar. 18, 1886.
19. Hoy letter to Kelker, Aug. 6, 1886; Moore, *Forty Years*, p. 75.
20. Moore, *Forty Years*, p. 77-94.
21. *The Messenger*, May 25, 1887.
22. Miller, *A History*, p. 29.
23. Hoy letter to Kelker, May 19, 1887.
24. *Ibid.*, Sept. 12, 1887; Hoy letter to Board, Nov. 13, 1887.
25. *The Messenger*, Nov. 23, 1887.
26. Hoy letter to Board, Sept. 21, 1887.
27. *Ibid.*, Oct. 6, 1887.

28. Hoy letter to Kelker, Nov. 13, 1887.
29. Hoy letter to Board, Nov. 13, 1887.
30. *Ibid.*, Nov. 24, 1887.
31. Schwartz letter to Kelker, Nov. 26, 1887.
32. Poorbaugh letter to Kelker, Nov. 1, 1887.
33. Ault letter to Kelker, Dec. 10, 1887.
34. *Ibid.*, Jan. 1888; *The Messenger*, Feb. 22, 1888.
35. Hoy letter to Board, Dec. 5, 1887.
36. *Ibid.*, Nov. 6, 1887.
37. *Ibid.*, Feb. 4, 1888.
38. *Ibid.*, Feb. 25, 1888.
39. *Ibid.*, Mar. 31, 1888.
40. *Ibid.*, Mar. 20, 1888.
41. *Ibid.*, Nov. 10, 1888.

Chapter V - BEGINNING OF CREATIVE TENSION

"The only form in which I beg is that you not misunderstand me." March 31, 1888

Hoy was a determined, stubborn fighter who never hesitated going ahead even on his own with whatever he deemed necessary. This had been his practice from the beginning when he had founded the Training School without Board help. Amidst the pressing needs to expand the work he became even more aggressive. Though he always acted in consultation with his missionary colleagues, the Board was often not happy with his bold initiative because it was put in the position where it could only comply or censure him. Hoy was also not intimidated by his youth in confronting churchmen of high position many of whom were twice his age. The foreign missionary movement from its inception had been championed, especially overseas, by undaunted young men and women like the Hoys, and then supported by their faithful elders back home like Kelker. In the process, which was sometimes painful for all concerned, the work progressed, practices were tested and policies evolved.

A fundamental problem with important implications for the future was raised by the difficulties in planning the building for the Girls' School. This was the Mission's first experience in constructing a building, for up until that time all the property had either been rented or purchased, with the buildings intact. Hoy submitted to the Board a plan designed by a foreign architect in Yokohama named Sarda which was rejected. One objection was that it had no cellar. Kelker submitted a design drawn up in Harrisburg with which neither Hoy nor Poorbaugh were pleased. Hoy replied.

> It misses the mark badly, and to one in Japan is almost funny. You either learn to respect and take our plans and opinions, or else send some one of your number you can trust. Your new plans show great ignorance of Japanese life. A little reflection ought to show any candid mind that it is impossible for anyone in America who has never lived in Japan to prepare an intelligent plan for school buildings. Japan is Japan, and America is America.[1]

The difficulties persisted. Two months later Hoy wrote, "Foreign female teachers and Japanese girls cannot use the same dining room and kitchen. Japanese diet and cooking are entirely different. Four instead of three recitation halls are needed. We could have planned better on the field, but let's not quarrel."[2] For Hoy and Poorbaugh their model school, both in terms of physical facilities and curriculum, was the Ferris Seminary in Yokohama.

High on Hoy's agenda had been also proper missionary housing. With the Board failing to respond to his continuing pleas, a few months after his marriage he informed Kelker that he would build his own house.

> I do not involve you in a single cent. If you choose to help me, well and good, but I do not want a single disputed penny to be put in my house. I will trust you to do the fair thing in annual rent. I am simply sick in body and mind and heart of begging. A better

house I must and will have. I have suffered enough by living three winters in a Japanese house, and I will not add a fourth winter. The Mission is with me in this. The only form in which I will beg is that you not misunderstand me.³

But Hoy had written without knowing that a week before the Board had adopted plans for a "combined school building and double dwelling house for Hoys and Schneders." Kelker also admonished Hoy, "Once for all, the Board wishes to make you comfortable. We have heard all we want to know about Japanese houses, and regret that they are so uncomfortable."⁴

Next Hoy turned to the needs of his little Training School. In August 1888 he informed the Board that with the approval of his colleagues he had bought with $1000 of his own money part of the lot owned by the Sendai Church and that in memory of his wife's father he would erect a building. Also, the property, valued at about $2,500, would be "held forever by a Japanese Board of Trustees in the interest of the Union Church." From the Board he expected only rent, but if at any time the Board wished to buy the property, he would charge no interest. "Have I done wrong? I can plead only my love for this school and my sincere desire to help our work."⁵

This bold initiative, so typical of Hoy, was in response to the urgent need of the growing school for more adequate quarters than the two rooms in the temple-church. That summer, largely due to the influence of Schneder, although the latter gave the credit to Oshikawa, a four-year preparatory course was added to the three-year theological program. This new curriculum consisted of mathematics, natural science, political economy, logic, psychology and ethics plus sufficient English to enable the students to pursue their theological studies in that language because the texts then were overwhelmingly in English. In fact, this latter consideration was one of the basic reasons for inaugurating the new approach. Also the number of students had increased to twenty-five. All new students were put on probation for four months during which time they had to support themselves. If financially supported either by congregations or individual church people in America, they had to agree to serve the Union Church for five years or repay the money. Also that fall a formal relationship between the Miyagi Classis and the school was established, and a constitution was adopted providing for a Board of Directors, composed of four missionaries and four Japanese. Thus the Sendai Theological Training School became an organic part of the Union Church of Christ in Japan.[6]

When Hoy learned that the Board had objections about the Ault Memorial he was deeply hurt. The reasons stated were that the building should be erected on the Board-owned lot next to the Girls' School, and that the property should have been given to the Board. Hoy vigorously defended his action and the policy behind it.

> Let no one question my motives. My purpose in giving to the native brethren instead of the Board is one of special interest in the progress and fortunes of the Japanese Church. The Japanese are by no means children, and I believe it is wrong for foreigners to hold all

the property. One half of the virtue of giving is lost if you still hold the deed of that which you profess to have given. This is the first case in Japan. All other Christian schools are owned by foreigners, that is, a Board. Can anyone censure me for taking more interest in the Japanese Church than in the Board ? Though I love the Board, I love the Japanese Church more.[7]

Some of the reactions against him were petty, even though sincere. In the same letter he commented on "an influential Board member who took me to task for doing an injustice to Mrs. Hoy by not laying up what little money I had against a future day. Why, Mrs. Hoy was and is the inspiration of my giving." In his next letter a month later he continued.

> I protest against this kind of treatment. Mrs. Hoy is now in tears. Is this the way the Bible teaches men to encourage one another in the Lord ? In the name of God, don't let this kind of treatment go too far. We have trials out here you know not of. None but a missionary can know. Don't add to our cares, for Jesus' sake. In very truth, by giving this gift to the Union Church in Japan, we have followed only the general principles by which you yourselves are working in and for the United Church in Japan. The only comfort Mrs. Hoy and I have in our relations with you now is in knowing that this unkind and unfair treatment comes, not from your hearts, but from your misunderstanding of our situation out here.[8]

Hoy's colleagues were not slow in coming to his defence. Poorbaugh, at the end of a long letter to Kelker wrote,

I feel sorry that there should have been any misunderstanding of Mr. Hoy's motives on the part of the Board in regard to giving the Training School and lot to the Japanese. Mr. Hoy may lack the wisdom that comes from experience but I am fully persuaded that there never was a missionary whose heart is more in his work or who devotes himself to it with greater singleness of purpose. To those who are about him daily, Mr. Hoy's purposes are as easily discerned as a man's thoughts possibly can be, and I know that the idea of superseding the Board is the farthest removed from his thoughts. For the sake of converting the Japanese, he would go without necessary food and clothing if his friends would let him. I think he is a little too enthusiastic in his idea of the extent to which the Japs should have their sense of their own dignity fostered, rather the way in which foreigners should foster it. In giving the boys' school to the Japanese, he has anticipated what we think will be a common thing a few years hence. Missionaries all look forward to transferring everything to the Japanese at no very distant day....<u>It will not be long before the people can take care of their own mission work</u>. We are rather conservative on this point, but many of the missionaries think that within the next ten years this change will take place.

Perhaps I've written more on this subject than I should, but it has seemed lately that Mr. Hoy has caused himself to seem a man somewhat like, or in cooperation with, Mr. Gring in his antagonism to the Board, which is so far from his real attitude I could not forbear writing as I have.[9]

Schneder, who had been elected secretary of the Japan Mission just five days after his arrival in Sendai the year before, also added in one of his regular communications with the Board that Hoy's gift should not have been given to the Board "because the school is owned not by foreigners but belongs to the Japanese." He also insisted that the new building should not be on the lot next to the Girls' School because "the close proximity of a large number of young men to a large number of young ladies would be a stumbling block and a rock of offence." He went on to chide the Board for not publicizing Hoy's sacrificial gift at home, which up to date was the largest individual contribution to foreign missions in the Reformed Church. "I do not understand why this noble act of a devout missionary should be condemned by faint praise." In closing he assured the Board that he had written only because "the suffering and tears of a dear and noble brother had moved me to it."[10] Furthermore, the Japan Mission at its regular meeting on October 6, 1888 had passed a resolution thanking the Hoys for their generous gift.

Yet the difficulty between the Board and Hoy continued. In yet another epistle, after confiding that he was having trouble sleeping, Hoy wrote,

> I need not tell you that I am thoroughly in love with these people and my work among them. It is just for this reason that the peculiar attitude of the Board toward the Ault Memorial Hall cuts me to the quick. If the Board can get any scriptural ground for their present attitude, then I have been reading my Bible wrong. Don't you know that we must blush from very shame before the Japanese to think that the Board loves itself more than it does the promising converts. Know you not that these children of a new faith are begotten of God, born of God? Some day, Dear Brethren, when you all learn my heart

you will rejoice that I did what I did and that I did it unto these
"blessed little ones." In the meantime this pain, this real spiritual
pain, will have its course and leave its traces, but God forbid that any
ill will should remain.[11]

The situation was complicated by other difficulties. Hoy and
Schneder had been pressing for a building for the Training School.
The June 15, 1888 issue of *The Messenger* had carried a plea from Hoy
for $3,000 for a Memorial Building in the name of whoever gave it.
"Isn't there one member of our Reformed Church who has the ability
and grace to pay for the Theological Seminary in Sendai ?" But the
Board was trying to raise $1,500 through special pledges in order to
send another missionary couple to Yamagata to help the Moores. Such
funds were duly received, although the appointee, a Rev. Schwedes,
soon withdrew and no one was sent, for by that time the money was
needed for other commitments.[12] In November *The Messenger*
published a long article by Schneder promoting the Training School
and describing the Ault Memorial which was nearing completion.
Then two weeks later the journal printed an Open Letter to the Board
from Hoy appealing for $5,000 for another building, the Oshikawa
Memorial.

Brother Oshikawa is one of the ablest and most eloquent
preachers in Japan. His preaching has reached and converted more
souls than that of any other minister in Japan. In him lies yet many
hopes for the speedy conversion of the north of Japan. Let us erect
this memorial building to his honor and as a mark of love and

appreciation. He is one of God's noblemen.[13]

Hoy's plea had been inspired by the gift of a widow in Ohio, who had heard about the gift of the widow in Sendai. This Hoy held up as an example for others back home to follow.[14] At the same time funds for the seminary were being raised by the Japanese. But the Board had reservations, especially because it did not welcome anything that seemed to be an independent solicitation by individual missionaries. Hoy was quick to correct the Board.

> If from mistaken ideas the Board takes pains to crush a spontaneous movement, no one can foresee the disaster, for certain liberal men are expressing liberal ideas here with the touch of real substantial gold. Dear Brother, I had rather lost my right hand than to receive the cruel suspicions of the Board. But I had rather be wronged than to be wrong. I am not making solicitations of funds, nor am I in sympathy with anyone that does so in a private way. Only mark this, the people will respond.[15]

In a separate letter the following day on a variety of matters he added, "The Ault building is a very substantial Japanese structure, said to be one of the best in Sendai." It was a two-story frame structure with seven classrooms and modest Japanese-style living quarters. Completed about the same time were the two missionary residences, one for the Hoys at Nibancho and the other for the single women at Sanbancho. Most impressive was the new Girls' School building, a handsome three story frame building with classrooms and dormitory, with an enrollment of forty-nine.

A more vexing difficulty was the one posed by Gring who was openly opposing the Training school, maintaining that the Union Seminary in Tokyo was sufficient and that the limited resources should be devoted to direct evangelism. As the first returned missionary he was being widely welcomed in the churches and his activities regularly reported in *The Messenger* by the most appreciative Board Secretary, Bartholomew. He was an able and convincing speaker who did much to promote the cause. His first summer on furlough he had taken Schneder with him to raise from the churches the money necessary to send the Schneders. But with the shift in Board policy toward increased involvement in education, Gring was becoming quite critical, and in the churches there were those who applauded his conservative approach.

Gring was a complex person, an enigma to his missionary colleagues and the Board. His trouble with the Board had started at least two years before his furlough, when he bitterly complained that his salary of $1,200 was insufficient and that if he were not given a furlough he would leave. He had criticized Mrs. Moore, and also the Board for appointing her, because she was "having an infatuation with a Japanese man," and was "losing her mind."[16] Kelker had evidently asked Hoy to check out Gring after his arrival in Japan, but Hoy had only commented in one of his first letters, "Let the dead bury the dead."[17] Poorbaugh in one of her first letters had written, "Mr. Gring has been exceedingly kind to us in our getting settled in Sendai, but the poor fellow makes a painful impression on one. Frail in appearance, he seems to me at times like a man whose intellectual powers are gradually slipping away from him." With apologies she added, "but my strong yearning over his pitiful condition moved me to say this." Gring's colleagues, however, had been supportive of him until well after his return to America, although when he had persisted in his intent to leave without Board approval, Hoy had advised him to be patient and let the Mission overture the Board in his behalf, which it did.[19]

The first note of open conflict came in the summer of 1888. The Board had asked Gring, who had been on furlough for more than a year, to return to Japan. Instead, without permission he had gone to London in June to attend an international missionary meeting. Hoy was bold enough to ask the Board if it was true that Gring had obtained from the Board $175 for the trip "on a false plea of poverty" and that he had left without "providing properly for his family."[20] In closing with the comment, "Has he come to this?" Hoy revealed his pent up suspicions. When Gring returned, the Board asked him to come to Harrisburg on August 26th to a special meeting. This was also announced in *The Messenger* "because the Church is already aware that there is a difference of opinion between the Board and its senior missionary." A later issue frankly reported,

> The most comfortable oil of unity did not flow. It was a question of principle and policy, and by no means one of prejudice and passion. The result would have been the resignation of the Board or of Gring. Gring will go forth for a year to speak in the

churches. It is the sincere wish of the Board as well as its missionaries that the past will be forgotten in the light of the present and in the prospects of the future.[21]

A break had been averted but in the process the entire church had been alerted to the fact that all was not well in its foreign mission enterprise which was not yet a decade old.

A related issue of contention worth recording concerned the use of the money from the sale of Gring's house in Tokyo after the decision to concentrate on Sendai had been made. The Board had expected more than the $3,000 it had brought, which led Hoy to chide, "It seems singular that men distant 8,500 miles from Tokyo should claim to know the value of property out here. Missionaries are going out into the country and there isn't much demand for houses in the foreign concession."[22] At its July 1888 meeting the Japan Mission had moved that the money be used for the Training School building,[23] but the Board needed the funds for the Girls' School building and for the missionary residences. This led Hoy to comment to Kelker, "If that money were put into some of our dwellings, Brother Gring would always delight in casting it up at us. It would be personally unpleasant to have Mr. Gring tell us that his house, as he calls it, had to be sold to build our houses. Do you think that he will return to Japan ? We fail to understand his moves. We must soon decide about the propriety of Gring's return to our Mission."[24] Kelker's letters were consistently supportive of the Japan Mission and increasingly candid about Gring. In commenting on Gring's suggestion that it would be better to send another family to Yamagata and abandon the Girls' School in Sendai he wrote, "I don't think this is worth listening to. The Sendai schools are our schools and the Yamagata school is not. In my humble judgment it was a foolish step to send a preacher of the Gospel to teach Japanese boys the English language six hours a day and expect him to do evangelistic work besides."[25] Later he admitted that the Board revenues were diminished "due to Gring's friends who are more concerned for the man than for the cause." There was no need to worry about Gring returning to Japan because "our Board has no money now to send him or anyone. As to what Brother Gring may say about our using the proceeds of the Tokio house in the Sendai buildings, you need not care. The Board is not amenable to him. We need no missionary Bishop or Superior to reside at the Capital of the Empire."[26] Yet "the Gring trouble" as it came to be known, coincided with a most crucial time of much needed expansion of the work in Sendai, especially with respect to the development of the Training School. It also aggravated misunderstandings which took much time to clarify by mail. In the late spring of 1888 the Japan Mission became so alarmed that it passed a resolution insinuating that the Board lacked confidence in the Mission, which Kelker was quick to assure Hoy was not true.[27]

Just as all of these difficulties were converging at the end of 1888, a most unfortunate miscommunication occurred between the Mission and the Board. In retrospect it was comical, but at the time it was irritating to all concerned. The missionaries were eager for Oshikawa to visit America to promote interest in the work as well as his own development. Also he was in poor health and needed a rest which was impossible for him in Japan. The fathers both of Hoy and Poorbaugh had agreed to take care of him, and the Board was sympathetic though its funds were scarce. Some money could be raised in Sendai, but more was needed. Hoy finally received a cable, "Send Oshikawa," to which he replied, "Thanks." But the Board had really cabled, "Don't send Oshikawa," and interpreted Hoy's reply as sarcastic.[28] After this misunderstanding was clarified by mail, the Japan Mission at its February 1889 meeting urged the Board to reconsider its decision which would offend both Oshikawa and his friends and harm the work.[29] According to Poorbaugh, Oshikawa was an invalid. "With heathenism all around him his spiritual zeal is consuming his vital forces." She went on to inform the Board that the Congregationalists had a plan whereby they sent their evangelists to America, and that if they didn't do the same they might lose Oshikawa who would "take with him all or nearly all of the work we have reported as ours. All of us together have not as much influence as Rev. Oshikawa who is almost without question the first native preacher in the empire."[30] The Board agreed and Oshikawa left for America in March at the Board's expense.

These converging difficulties came to a climax early in 1889. The Japan Mission passed a resolution censuring Kelker and the Board, although the resolution itself is not in the records. Kelker wrote to Hoy, "Don't listen to Gring. I don't feel censured." Three weeks later in responding to a letter from Hoy, Kelker insisted that Hoy was misinformed in his reaction to the Board's position concerning the Ault Memorial. Hoy should name the men on the Board who were critical of him. "The official action of the Board is more for enquiry than for censure, for as a Board or individuals we have no right to interfere in any way with your benevolent intentions." In reasoning for the Board ownership of the property he argued that Mary's father had been a pastor of the Reformed Church and that the Union Church was not as appropriate a recipient. As to the request for $5,000 for the seminary, "We do not have the means to build it and a Girls' School plus two houses in one year. I asked you to wait and not build your house at your own expense, which might in case of your death be an embarrassment to your wife. The Church intended to build a house for you." But he ended on a reassuring note. "I know of no Board member that has not the greatest confidence in you. I have not ceased to do everything I could to make you happy and to remember you in my prayers. I am only a servant of the Board. You are justly regarded as the founder of the seminary and your sacrifices made in founding it fully appreciated."[31]

Several months later Hoy apologized to the Board for "being misinformed." He was "thankful for their forebearance and regrets any pain he has caused." He added, "We know too well what Brother Gring has caused you in pain and in money, but no one in the Mission is a personal enemy of Brother Gring's."[32] On the same day he wrote more fully to Kelker,

> By outside influence I have been led on several occasions to pass some harsh criticisms on the Board in letters to Brother Bartholomew and Dr. Weiser. I see now that I was misinformed and regret any

pain I may ever have caused the Board. I am sorry for some things I have said to the Board. I now wonder at, and am grateful for, the forebearance of the Board. I can assure you that the whole Mission is now at one with the Board, and not one of your missionaries has any sympathy whatever with those in the Church who now cry out against you. We know too well what Brother Gring has caused you in pain and in money. And again, no one in the Mission is a personal enemy of his. God forbid that we should be actuated by feelings of enmity.[33]

Yet scars remained which accentuated later difficulties with the Board.

On June 5, 1889 Mary was delivered of her first child a month late by forceps which took its life. They named their son, Carl Whitmer, and buried him in the little Christian section of the cemetery of Rinnoji Zen Temple (the Temple of the Reincarnation) near the grave of the Schneder's first baby, John, who had died the year before at birth.[34] Oshikawa had been instrumental in procuring that first Christian burial plot.

In America Oshikawa was being well received not only because he was the first Japanese from the Mission of the Reformed Church in Japan to make such a visit but also because of his many abilities which included fluency in English. He was obviously a most exotic attraction with things to say which few of his listeners had ever heard. Kelker wrote to Hoy, "We are delighted with Oshikawa. He is now at your parents' home. We are a thousand times thankful that Providence allowed the telegraph operator to omit the word 'not' in Dr. Weiser's cablegram."[35] The Board Secretary, Bartholomew, wrote a short biography of Oshikawa entitled, *Won by Prayer*, which was published by the Reformed Church Press. Widely circulated in the churches, it represented the first book concerning its Japan Mission with the proceeds designated for the Seminary. Oshikawa himself was forthright in promoting the work. But when Hoy learned that his colleague wanted to raise $20,000 for another church, he advised the Board that $5,000 would be enough and that the needs of the seminary should come first."[36]

Despite the difficulties Hoy remained undaunted in promoting "the Seminary" as it was coming to be known. In *The Messenger*, April 4, 1889, he wrote,

> In December two of our first students appeared before the Sendai Classis for licensure, and they are now preaching the Gospel. I wish you could see "our boys." You would certainly love them all. How they love to pray. They all rise at half past five and hold a prayer meeting of thirty minutes. In the evening they again assemble for prayer, and every Friday evening Brother Schneder and I meet with them and give a practical talk on some phase of the religious life.

Hoy saw the seminary in Sendai as "the Key to the North of Japan." In order to start building in 1890 he urged the Board to borrow the money immediately and offered to pay the interest on the loan himself.[37] He was happy to report that the Miyagi Classis was raising money for the seminary and that the students were contributing fifty cents monthly to the Seminary Fund, which by June totaled $1525. "To raise a strong native ministry is our best work. Let us build the

Oshikawa Memorial Seminary next year."[38] He and Schneder were full of dreams and plans for the school. They proposed naming the chapel after the President of the Board, Rev. T.S. Johnston, and the library after the treasurer, Mr. Rudolph Kelker. A plan was also proposed for raising money in the Sunday Schools at home. The first prize would be an Album of Japan Scenes; the second prize, four volumes entitled "Japan in Days of Yore;" third prize, a Japanese embroidered cushion cover; fourth prize, a Japanese idol; and fifth prize, chop sticks. In presenting this plan Hoy concluded by urging the Board, as he often did, to be more business-like. "Here is room for a little business." This project was warmly recommended by the Board to the people of the churches through *The Messenger*. In fact, almost every issue of that weekly publication contained articles on the Seminary as well as about Oshikawa and his various activities.[39]

Where financial responsibility was concerned even in small matters Hoy did not hesitate to advance the money himself with the hope of being reimbursed, as he always was. He paid the $262.50 for Oshikawa's passage so he could sail without delay, as well as $140 for the tuition for two girls in "Miss Lette's school in Tsukiji." Gring had raised the scholarships from churches at home, but the money from the churches was no longer being received. Gring had done this independently, so the Board was not officially responsible and felt that such scholarships should be used for girls in the Sendai school. Yet Hoy felt responsibility for the girls in Tsukiji, who later transferred to Sendai. The Board eventually credited Hoy's account for the total of $302.50, with Hoy reminding them that he had acted "for the honor of the Mission" and that he could "not afford to lose the money."[40] This also reveals how tight the Mission treasury was at that time.

Meanwhile "the Gring trouble" was reaching a climax. The Board had asked the Schneders to replace the Moores in Yamagata, because their health was failing, and Gring was designated to take Schneder's place at the seminary. The Japan Mission replied that the loss of Schneder and addition of Gring "would cripple and perhaps ruin the school." Gring had conditioned his return upon having a western house, and the Board had authorized him to raise the $2,500 needed. But by the time of the Board meeting on April 24th only two thirds of the money had been pledged and only one third received. Also the Yamagata authorities had just notified the Mission that they would no longer support the school financially and it was clear the Board could not assume the full financial responsibility. Oshikawa, who was present at the Board meeting in Harrisburg, had urged the priority of the seminary as the basis of evangelistic work through the training of a native ministry. It was, therefore, decided that there was "no need for another missionary" and that "the treasury does not warrant sending one." The result was the resignation of Gring effective May 1st, which was duly reported in *The Messenger* along with thanks to Gring for his eight years of faithful service. This was followed a week later by an Open Letter written by the Board President, Dr. Z. C. Weiser, to reassure the readers that the reasons for Gring's termination were financial and not personal. Two weeks later a longer letter from Bartholomew, the Board Secretary, explained in detail the changed circumstances which had advised against sending Gring or any missionary at that time and the need to develop the seminary instead. "We love Brother Gring but we love the cause of Christ more. There are times in the history of the Church when the individual must drop out for the general good." Gring was circulating an Open Letter which was finally printed in *The Messenger*, July 31st, insisting that he had not resigned but been dismissed, and that the reasons were not just financial but personal in ways injurious to his character. He asked the Board to affirm publicly that there were no such other reasons or state plainly what they were.[41] This brought forth another lengthy Open Letter signed by all eleven members of the Board in the September 11th issue of *The Messenger* stating quite candidly that Gring was disaffected toward Board policy, insubordinate in his relationships, and extravagant with mission funds. "Experience shows he should have been recalled five years ago. Some of the most liberal supporters among our ministers who know the circumstances declared their unwillingness to continue their support if he were returned, while others demanded his return." With this the long-standing sorry affair was rather fully exposed. Kelker had written to Hoy that Gring's resignation was providential but that there were repercussions.

> Some of Gring's personal friends in the ministry will use his resignation as an excuse to withhold their support of the Board for some time, until they have learned of his misconduct toward the Board, his insubordination and extravagance. He has had his friends to get resolutions passed by Gettysburg, East Pennsylvania and Maryland Classis, asking the Board to reinstate him and censure the Board.[42]

A week earlier Hoy had written that Gring had tried to get the missionaries to side with him. "Not one of us is at all a personal enemy of Gring, but we think that we can get along best without him in Sendai, and we hope the Church sustains the Board."[43]

Among Gring's supporters, Dr. J. S. Kieffer of the Potomac Classis contributed an article to the June 19, 1889 *Messenger* in defence of Gring's accomplishments and his conservative philosophy of mission, arguing that schools were too expensive for the limited resources of the Reformed Church, that the Union Seminary in Tokyo was sufficient for the educational needs and that the funds should be used for direct evangelism. This was answered a month later by an official explanation from the Board Secretary in order to counter the opposition without mentioning Gring by name or the Classis involved.[44] The controversy continued with *The Messenger* giving coverage to both sides although support of Gring was confined to considerations of mission policy. The November 13th issue carried an article signed by "S" who argued that the seminary in Sendai would promote denominationalism. This "S" must have been the Dr. Srangler identified by Hoy as one of Gring's friends who "is striking at the Seminary. Our school will strengthen the Union. Take this school from us, if Mr. Gring's men are to prevail, and you may as well take us from Japan. It is the working base for our Mission. Let me remind you that we were invited by the Union Church to occupy Sendai for the very purpose of engaging in school work."[45] The controversy was clarifying the role of education in evangelism and quite ironically had rallied the Board to promote its schools in Sendai, especially the much neglected Training School. The Board began promoting the Oshikawa Memorial Fund, and in February *The Messenger* printed the first of four long articles by Schneder about the school. Yet mission finances, which had never been good, were suffering. Hoy asked Kelker, "We fail to see why the Church is falling back on her contributions, why one man should come between her and God's course. Yet we are confident that the Church will come to its senses."[46]

In January 1890 Gring asked the Board to return his resignation, which the Board promptly refused to do. Kelker assured Hoy, "Our Board will never send Gring back under any circumstances. If General Synod would direct us to do so after our experience with him, every one of us would resign at once."[47] To the Board Hoy wrote,

> We have found Gring out. As soon as he resigned from the services of our Board he began in a secret and unprincipled way to work against our seminary. He has himself to blame that the Mission has now utterly lost all faith in his manliness. He struck at us in the dark, and we and the Union Council have found him out.[48]

The movement against the seminary, moreover, was losing its momentum. The climax for Gring came when he submitted a memorial to General Synod at its meeting from May 28 to June 6 at Lebanon, Pennsylvania, requesting it to "appoint a committee to investigate all matters relating to my missionary trust and if said charges are found to be groundless to exonerate me of them." The committee, headed by the venerable Dr. Thomas G. Apple, Professor of Church History at Lancaster Seminary, held eight meetings of three hours each, at which both the Board and Gring were examined. The committee decided that the action of the Board concerning the resignation was beyond its scope, and the relationship between Gring and the Board was so incompatible that there was no other alternative, but that no reflection against Gring's character was intended or implied. Within a few months the Grings joined the Episcopal Church with the hope of returning to Japan.[49]

Despite all the difficulties, Hoy, with the help of Schneder, kept pressing the Board for the new seminary building, insisting that the problem wasn't just Gring but the church itself, and that if the Reformed Church people gave in the same proportion as the Japanese Christians, there would be sufficient funds. When in defence the Secretary had used the word "sacrifice" Hoy retorted, "Sacrifice in America is put to blush by these poor Christians in Japan who sell the very coats off their backs. Sacrifice is what sacrifice does."[50] In the fall of 1889 when the Training School had to turn down applicants, Hoy passionately appealed through *The Messenger* "To the Sunday School Scholars," asking them to give five cents each for the new building.

> The other day a poor young man walked all the way from Tokyo to enter our school. He was very tired, and poor boy, we had to refuse his application. We have no room for him. He has been begging for a week to be admitted into the school. It caused me a

great deal of pain tonight to turn him off again. These young men are waiting. We are waiting. The Lord is waiting.[51]

In response a church in Ohio decided not to have a Christmas tree that year and give the money to the Seminary Fund. But since much more was needed Hoy, in his characteristic way, proposed boldly to the Board.

> If the Gring trouble continues to interfere with the prospects of the seminary so that the Reformed Church will not give us the means to build in the spring of 1890, I propose, with your sanction and prayers, to erect the needed building myself. It will be a heavy burden for me, but I have prayed to the Lord and am not afraid of hard toil. God helps him who helps himself. I have learned to wait when waiting is virtue, but in this case the growth of the school and the spiritual blessedness of the hopes and promises that center in these young men now preparing for the ministry to not allow me to wait. Brethren, I have had enough business experience to know that I can do what the Lord points out. Let me know by cable, the cost of cable to my account, by February 10, 1890.[52]

The Japan Mission at its meeting two weeks later recommended going ahead with the building to cost $5,000 with Hoy responsible for the payments until the Board funds were forthcoming. It also recommended building a house for the Schneders and that all the property be owned and controlled jointly by the Mission Board and the Japanese Board of Trustees.[53] Hoy also implored the Board to send out another teacher for the seminary, a single man in case there was not enough money for a family. He and his wife would board him for $250 a year and surely some church at home would pay the passage.[54] Meager resources were never considered a reason for not pressing forward with the work.

Footnotes

1. Hoy letter to Board, Jan. 25 and Feb. 3, 1888.
2. *Ibid.*, Mar. 31, 1888.
3. *Ibid.*, Mar. 31, 1888.
4. Kelker letter to Hoy, Feb. 3, 1888.
5. Hoy letter to Board, Aug. 3, 1888 and next undated letter.
6. *The Messenger*, Feb. 13, 1890.
7. Hoy letter to Board, Dec. 16, 1888.
8. *Ibid.*, Feb. 23, 1889.
9. Poorbaugh letter to Kelker, Jan. 15, 1889.
10. Schneder letter to Board, Feb. 2, 1889.
11. Hoy letter to Board, Feb. 18, 1889.
12. *The Messenger*, Mar. 14 and Mar. 23, 1888.
13. *Ibid.*, Nov. 28, 1888.
14. *Ibid.*, Dec. 12, 1888 and Letter to Board, Oct. 14, 1888.
15. Hoy letter to Board, Feb. 11 and 12, 1889.
16. Gring letter to Board, Jan. 2, 1885.
17. Hoy letter to Kelker, Feb. 8, 1886.
18. Poorbaugh letter to Kelker, July 29, 1886.
19. *Ibid.*, Oct. 23 and Nov. 3, 1886.
20. Hoy letter to Board, Aug. 26, 1888.
21. *The Messenger*, July 11 and Sept. 5, 1888.
22. Hoy letter to Board, Nov. 24, 1887.
23. Mission Proceedings, July 1888.

24. Hoy letter to Kelker, June 21 and Aug. 21, 1888.
25. Kelker letter to Hoy, Feb. 3, 1888.
26. *Ibid.*, May 18, July 16, Aug. 22, 1888.
27. *Ibid.*, June 30, 1888.
28. Hoy letter to Board, Feb. 5, 1893.
29. Mission Proceedings, Feb. 1889.
30. Poorbaugh letter to Kelker, Jan. 15, 1889.
31. Kelker letter to Hoy, Feb. 8 and 28, 1889.
32. Hoy letter to Board, July 20, 1889.
33. Hoy letter to Kelker, July 20, 1889.
34. *Ibid.*, June 11, 1889.
35. Kelker letter to Hoy, June 8, 1889.
36. Hoy letter to Board, July 23, 1889.
37. *Ibid.*, May 8, 1889.
38. *Ibid.*, April 4 and June 27, 1889.
39. *Ibid.*, July 15, 1889 and *Messenger*, Sept. 11, 1889.
40. Hoy letter to Kelker, May 17, 1889.
41. *The Messenger*, May 8, 15, 22, and July 31, 1889.
42. Kelker letter to Hoy, June 8, 1889.
43. Hoy letter to Kelker, June 13, 1889.
44. *The Messenger*, July 17, 1889.
45. Hoy letter to Board, Sept. 2, 1889.
46. Hoy letter to Kelker, Aug. 29 and Sept. 23, 1889.
47. Kelker letter to Hoy, Feb. 20 ; Gring letter to Board, May 28, 1889 Jan. 31 and Feb. 17, 1890.
48. Hoy letter to Board, Feb. 5, 1890.
49. Kelker letter to Hoy, Aug. 7, 1890 : *General Synod Tenth Triennial Meeting Proceedings 1890* and *The Messenger*, July 17, 1890.
50. Hoy letter to Board, Sept. 23, 1889 and Feb. 25, 1889.
51. *Ibid.*, Oct. 15, 1889 and Jan. 17, 1890.
52. *Ibid.*, Dec. 6, 1889.

53. Mission Proceedings, Dec. 18, 1889.
54. Hoy letter to Board, Nov. 3, 1889.

Chapter VI - BEGINNING OF REACTION

"Is not the Gospel deep enough to comprehend us all ? Is the morbid phrase, My Country, more comprehensive than The Kingdom of Our Father ?" June 6, 1891

By the end of 1889 the Mission Board was in such financial distress that it couldn't send sufficient funds on time to the Japan Mission to meet its regular expenses. As treasurer, Hoy borrowed "to cover the delinquencies of the Board and Church." Also the depreciation of silver had brought a loss of $1500 by February. To Bartholomew he wrote,

> I work from 5 a.m. to 9 p.m. We have no strength reserved to bear these new burdens thrust upon us by the Board and Church. Neither can you expect our self-denying Japanese co-laborers to go hungry and naked. The matter of daily bread is just as urgent in God's business as in any other vocation. Patience is no longer a virtue. We have done our part of the work faithfully. If the other party of the covenant proves unfaithful, we know what to do.[1]

Hoy was referring to the Articles of Agreement signed by the Board officials and the missionaries at the time of their appointment. What Hoy apparently then did not know was that Bartholomew and Kelker were also deeply distressed. An Open Letter to Pastors, Elders, and Members of the Reformed Church was published in the April 3, 1891 issue of *The Messenger* describing the gravity of the crisis and appealing for help, especially to "the vast number who have never sent in any contribution." In May the Board borrowed $5,000 "to enable us to pay our missionaries." Kelker wrote to Hoy, "This want of funds is owing to the baleful influence the conduct of Mr. Gring has had on the Church by misrepresenting us."[2] Yet there were other factors as noted by *The Messenger* in a later article. The crops had been damaged by the wet summer the year before and also much church money had gone to the victims of the flood of the Susquehanna River.[3] Yet the missionaries were convinced that the most important reason was the lethargy of many pastors and people concerning foreign missions. From Japan they did everything they could to awaken interest.

It wasn't until March 20th that Hoy received the long expected cable from the Board concerning the proposed seminary building which read "Build but await advice." In the interim plans drawn up both in Sendai and in Harrisburg were exchanged. With respect to the details of design this time the Board deferred to the Japan Mission with the stipulation that the total cost could not exceed $5,000, and that the building should be built on land belonging to the Board or on a part of the Ault lot to be purchased for a nominal price.[4] Again the problem was ownership.

> I hardly know what to say about the Board's desire to own what ought to be given directly to God's poor. Let the Board however be careful not to add to the growing antipathy to foreigners which is beginning to tell against Gospel work. To be honest, I think the desire to control the Japanese in compelling them to receive Christian gifts on trust in the name of a foreign company is both unscriptural and brings a barrier between natives and foreigners. I certainly

should spurn the gift of a man who would make me hold his gift to me as trust in his name. Oh, the very thought is so repugnant to me that I sometimes wish I had money enough of my own to plant the Kingdom of Christ in gifts of unconditioned love. God help us!⁵

In answering the cable on the day he received it, Hoy advised the Board that legally the property must be registered in a Japanese name and that Oshikawa had been his inspiration for giving his own gifts directly to "the natives." I can only pray that you may see the way clear to give your gifts to the Japanese at once without any formalities that smatter of silent distrust of the Japanese."⁶

In order to raise the money for the building the February 13th issue of *The Messenger* printed a "challenge for 20 men to give $200 for the seminary." Before Oshikawa sailed for Japan via Europe on January 31st, the Board voted to pay him a yearly salary of $700 which was equal to that of a single male missionary. In appreciation Schneder wrote, "The fact that he will hereafter be financially comfortable is a pleasure to me and the prospect that the relation between him and us will be permanent offers me much hope." Upon Oshikawa's return to Sendai, *The Messenger* printed the following tribute by Schneder. "When the ship that brought him back first bore him in sight of his native land, he wept. He wept for the material poverty of his country, wept for the moral and spiritual degradation. As a preacher and leader he has no equal. Since the death of Niijima, the foremost and most influential of Japanese Christians is Oshikawa."⁷

But Oshikawa had a tempting offer to go to Tokyo as Vice President of Union College and Hoy was afraid the seminary would lose him.

Referring to the loss in 1870 by Lancaster Seminary of one of America's eminent theologians, Hoy asked Bartholomew, "Why did Dr. Schaff leave the Reformed Church ? If the Reformed Church had been wise enough and active enough to give him opportunity to use his God-given genius, he would never have left us."[8] In the same letter he urged the Secretary, "Dear Brother, do not be offended when I say that you ought to give all your time to our cause. You cannot keep your congregation and at the same time succeed in your Foreign Mission office. The Board and the Church both need a little more experience of the burden of work outside of strife." Bartholomew, the pastor of a large church in Pottsville, Pennsylvania, resigned that fall and was replaced by the Rev. Samuel N. Callender, the first full-time executive of the Board. Also Rudolph F. Kelker retired, his beloved wife having just died. In her memory he donated an elegantly equipped library room with 282 volumes from America for the Girls' School. He had been a pillar in the foreign mission enterprise of the Reformed Church. It had been at his home in Harrisburg that the Foreign Board had been reorganized in 1873 and many meetings had been held in his spacious parlors.[9] His replacement by Joseph L. Lemberger brought inevitable changes, not least of which was the end of that special relationship of understanding and confidence which had existed between the treasurer of the Board and the treasurer of the Japan Mission. But for William and Mary Hoy the most immediate change at that time was the birth of William Edwin on August 23, 1890. In an article about the seminary in *The Messenger*, Hoy reported, "I must not forget to mention the arrival of one more seminary student. His name is William Edwin Hoy Jr. He handed in his application just four weeks ago, but on account of his tender age and uncertain character, his mother has put him on further probation."[10]

That summer all the missionaries except Hoy, who was busy with the building plans, were at the sea near Sendai. This is his first reference to Takayama, a lovely spot with towering pine covered cliffs and a sandy beach, which became a missionary vacation haven. To the Board Hoy revealed that he was buying a strip of land for $500 between the Ault Memorial and the Sendai Church, as a gift to the seminary, requesting that his name should not be mentioned. Also because of the devalued dollar the cost of the building had increased from $5,000 to $7,500.[11] For *The Messenger* he wrote a long and moving article about a seventeen-year-old girl whom he and Oshikawa had tried to rescue from being sold into prostitution by her poor parents.[12] Then he was shocked to learn that there had been no "foreign missions service" at the General Synod Meeting back home at the end of May. "This neglect shows too painfully how indifferent our Church is on this point. We must be more aggressive."[13] The construction of the new seminary began just before classes started that fall. Since it was to be a substantial western-style brick structure it required minute supervision, for which Hoy's boyhood training on the farm and his recent experience with the Girls' School had prepared him well. Sendai had few such buildings and the task was monumental. "No one without the experience can appreciate the amount of calking care involved in the erection of four buildings at one time in Japan," he had written the year before. "I am too tired to sleep."[14]

The student body of what Hoy and Schneder loved to call "The School of the Prophets" now numbered forty. Among the new students was the young man who had walked all the way from Tokyo the year before, only to be turned down because of lack of space. A lady in the 'Home Church' had provided him with a scholarship of $60, which was enough for one year. In a poignant appeal for more scholarships Hoy urged all those at home who had experienced the pain of losing a child, of whom there were then many, to have the joy of educating one of the seminary boys at far less the cost than in America.[15] Desperate for another missionary and the salary for one more Japanese teacher, he erupted, "I for one am not willing to labor much longer in this one-sided self-denial. I am constrained to feel that there must be some lack of confidence in us. I am weary of pleading. I have done enough of it privately and publicly. I leave the special efforts for the progress in the hands of the Board and the Church. May God save us all in our indifference to his Holy Cause."[16] He ended by commenting that the work in Japan was more difficult than when he arrived five years before.

Most urgent, however, was the fact that the money from the Board was not being received regularly. Finally at the end of December when the fall quarterly payment had not yet arrived he pleaded with Callender, the new secretary, for $8,599 by March.

> We can't beg or steal or be self-supporting as missionaries. If matters grow worse, we shall have to make the matter of our daily

bread our first and great concern. For that the Board and Church did not commission us. Both Board and Church must put forth sterner business effort or else withdraw the missionaries. Would to God I had a better subject for this letter, but this one has been thrust upon us by an unholy indifference on the part of the people who sent us forth. A change must be made at once.[17]

The Board, by no means unconcerned, was pressing hard for funds. Almost every issue of *The Messenger* documented its financial plight. In February the Secretary pleaded for $5,000, having just had to borrow that exact sum. "Funds are coming in so slowly that there is a necessary delay in remitting quarterly payments of salaries, to the embarrassment and hardship of the missionaries."[18] But the response was slow and most of the special gifts quite small. One man sent $5 with the explanation that when he had left his overcoat on the train he had vowed that if it were returned he would make a gift to the Seminary Fund.[19] From Rev. C.R. Ferner of Mt. Pleasant, Pa., $2,000 was received, three-fourths of which was used to purchase books for the Kelker Memorial Library in the new building.[20] In April the Board granted the furlough for the Moores which the Japan Mission had recommended, "because of the financial crisis, to promote the work among the churches."[21] Also the Moores had been in Japan eight years and Annie's health was poor. The June 25th issue of *The Messenger* carried a financial statement by Secretary Callender revealing that the Board was receiving only nine cents a year per member, that the Reformed Church with 203,000 members had raised only $18,000 for foreign missions the previous year, and that "Missionary Hoy" had already put from $4,000 to $5,000 of his own money into the seminary building under construction. Yet despite it all, a new missionary teacher for the Girls' School was appointed, Miss Mary C. Hollowell of Chambersburg, Pennsylvania,[22] under the auspices of the Women's Missionary Society.

Despite the many demands on time and energy, Hoy and his wife continued their work in direct evangelism, especially on week-ends with the seminarians helping them. When the church at Shiroishi baptized eighteen persons in 1899 Hoy exclaimed, "Souls are ready for the Jesus Way." His first mention of the beginnings in Nagamachi, which was then outside Sendai, was in April 1891 when he reported that "Mrs. Hoy's Sunday School has 130 students with an average attendance of 81 and two just baptized." According to Mary, her pupils were "very poor children many of whom come with only a thin ragged calico gown to cover their little limbs," so she asked the churches at home to send flannel to make underwear. "Nagamachi is a hard place for Christian work because the parents are against us." The Hoys also asked the Board for a "baby organ" for the work there. William also reported that he had organized three small Sunday Schools in the vicinity of Sendai and that in Shiroishi he had just baptized five men and two women, although evangelistic work is very slow now."[23]

Hoy's periodic reports to the Board about the seminarians on scholarships provided by the 'Home Church' reveal much about the students and the school. Out of the 14 such students in 1891, two,

Nishihara and Hashimoto, were licensed and in full time work. Abe left school early to start evangelistic work, but it was hoped that he would return when he realized his need for more study. Matsuda had returned after having left two years before, "an unfaithful and ungrateful young man who grew disobedient and impudent. We tried to bring him to repentance, but we gave up in dispair. He says he will repay, but this is doubtful." Kodaira, "much loved" had died, which was reported in a moving article in *The Mesenger*. Kurihara and Niiyama had been expelled and Muto had been dismissed because of his "mental incapacity." Ota, Yamada, and Shimanuki had become self supporting, the latter as an instructor in the school. Hagiwara, Nakamura, and Tamura, fully supported, were studying well. Not named were eight other self-supporting students and nine who were partially supported, bringing the total enrollment to thirty-one. This report occasioned the first of many requests for an English teacher, which were not met until the coming of Rev. Paul Gerhard in 1897.[18]

Hoy's incessant pleas for funds while the new seminary building was under construction precipitated a crisis between himself and the Board that spring of 1891. No record remains of the Board's position, but it evidently had concluded that Hoy wanted to be relieved of his voluntary financial responsibility for the payments in Sendai. It therefore had censured him with the order to suspend construction of the building. Hoy was quick to insist that the Board had completely misunderstood his intent and strongly requested it "to strike from your books those unjust and unkind actions relative to the seminary building and myself." He also pleaded for a better relationship with the

Board.

From the very beginning of my hard, hard work of building up this Seminary on my own private contributions, instead of common Christian love I have received nothing but a series of adverse and doubtful resolutions. But I need not repeat the past. At first I was unsophisticated enough to hope for sympathy from the Board, but after the bitter correspondence relative to the Ault Memorial I ceased to look for anything of the kind. I am not sick of our work, but God knows that I am weary of these unkind, unjust and thoughtless resolutions. If the Board cannot put implicit faith in me, let the statement be made in a straight forward way and not couched in evasive resolutions. I do not write this in anger. I simply want a better understanding and a little more just consideration. I do not flatter myself that the Mission could not go on without me. If I am growing so disagreeable to the Board, you had better either convert me to your methods or ask me to resign. Rest assured, dear Doctor, that I mean to do my duty to the Seminary as long as you own me as your servant. This precious School of the Prophets has my very heart's blood and I would never destroy one ray of her growing hope of great usefulness. An institution like the Sendai Theological Seminary is more than one man, and will increase with its years, though men may come and go.

I used to pray that God would give me something to do that no one else could or would do, and in these five years of intense struggle and heavy burdens, I have had the infinite pleasure (this is private) of contributing at least $5,000 to the Seminary. I am not a man of wealth. I have started out with the Gospel of Giving, *first* to the Lord and providing for my wants *secondly*. The results are simply marvelous. If I remember correctly I received the idea from one of the Wesleys. It is sweetly practical and works wonders as to results. The usual methods of providing first for self and secondly or thirdly for God, would land me in unbelief. The Lord must either come first in *all* things or else we have practically no place for God. I have no use for sentimental or doctrinal Christianity in my own life. Either God first and self second, or self first and bitter atheism for me. If I believe in Christ, I must also believe in Him. The usual interpretation put on Christ's words in relation to giving is a trick of the Devil, and is for me the temptation of all temptations. But I cannot hope to convert anyone to my view of Christ's injunctions in methods of giving. I simply state what I have found best for my own faith and peace. I do not feel strong enough to preach when the mere practice of my Gospel brings me naught but misunderstanding from others. I know from the very best evidence that a member of the Board has said that my practice is "a sin."[19]

Hoy's letter a month later on a completely different subject is worth quoting because it is such a poignant commentary about many things. The Board had listed Hoy as President of the Seminary, which he was, for all practical purposes, since Oshikawa was gone much of the time and not much interested or involved in administrative details. Hoy reminded the Board that he was only the vice-president and that the error should be corrected.

The Japanese brethren are very sensitive about these matters. Anything that seems like foreign rule or authority is obnoxious to them. Their "patriotism" is simply morbid, and the foreign missionary sometimes must bear with a great deal of questionable treatment. We cannot but think of the better relations that existed a few years ago. Foreign money is, however, never refused. Poor Japan! She is her own worst enemy. She has much to learn yet. We are perfectly willing to decrease and to have our Japanese brethren increase, but our hearts do occasionally crave a little more palpable fraternal love and regard. What is that subtle thing that makes racial distinction, race feelings, race prejudice? By what mysterious force are the Japanese Christians impelled, when simply for racial differences and national prejudice they ignore the tender ties that once bound them to the "foreign missionary." Is not the Gospel deep enough to comprehend us all? Is the morbid phrase "My Country" more comprehensive than "the Kingdom of our Father?" Some Japanese sermons have dozen words for "My Country" to one for "Our Father's House." Among the Japanese Christians we have some very dear and near friends, such as our beloved and trusted brother Oshikawa, but we often long for more intimate relations with some who have gone away into the stream of anti-foreign feeling.[21]

In a rare reference to family Hoy noted, "Our dear Willie grows sweeter and prettier every day. Of course, he is the Emperor enthroned in our little family. He was nine months old last Saturday."[81] There were three missionary children, Mary Schneder born on March 15th, the same year as Willie, and Kittie Poorbaugh, then age 11. Hoy also indicated that his health was breaking again and that early in July he and his family would go to the seashore for their "first real summer vacation. I must return, however, almost daily to oversee the completion of the seminary building."[22] His letter from Takayama to Secretary Callender is worth quoting in its entirety.

The waves call me and I long to take a cold plunge, and feel the big heart of life and force that throbs in and through the deep. Here lies a grain of sand torn from the parent rock, one knows not how, many miles away. A shell that was once a house beautiful for a creature dwelling at the bottom of the sea, delights my baby Willie. Some seaweed, curious in form and color and scent, finds its way into the herbarium as fondly collected by wife Mary. Baby shouts and claps his hands and for very joy of life hides his face in his mother's bosom. The waves rise and fall, beat and roll, seethe and foam, at the foot of the cliff. Three miles out at sea a large number of fishermen's boats may be seen riding the waves at will. In the blue expanse above lazily wings the seagull.

And now several miles out at sea in a small sailing vessel, a force we can feel and hear but neither see nor handle, drives us hither and thither, not, however, at its own sweet will, for the boatman wedded to wind and wave is master of both, and his skill puts us at ease. Resting, simply resting! Thinking, peacefully thinking! Dreaming, with a thrill and a divine impulse dreaming! God and Heaven, Earth and Regeneration, Christ and Righteousness, Japan and our Mission, Japan and our Home Church, Life and Love and Duty! And the boat leaps a high wave. Dreams are broken, but not committed to the deep, except the deep of a soul trusting in the God of Mission.

Baby Willie again tries to play with the sparkling foam on the crest of a wave. The Japanese boatman, seemingly enraptured with this little bud of life, smiles and sometimes laughs aloud at the movements of the child. Papa takes a glass and fills it with water from the great ocean. Willie's tiny hands are thrust into this glassful and rare sport is in store for the occupants of the boat. The clear blue sky above, the deep blue sea below, the boat, the sails, the boatman, to the left some thousands of miles away the old home and preparation for the world, to the right within sight, Japan and work present and future. Now floating with the gentle breeze, and we are resting with heart and mind full of beautiful things, things old and new, things of sea, things of sky, things of earth, things of Heaven, things of and for Japan, things of hope and work, a treasury that may enrich at least one soul.

Christ among the fishermen of old gave power that made men fishers of men. When will the thousands and thousands of Japanese fishermen know Christ? How many Peters here? How many Johns? From among the most ignorant of the Japanese may we look for a herald of the Gospel? Here in Japan an unlettered fisherman would need power divine to meet the pride of intellect so dominant at present. In God's time from these lowly men may come a voice that shall be heard throughout Japan. Not in pride and not in strength, not in intellect merely and not in birth or rank, not in philosophy and not in science, will the Great Preacher of Japan trust when he arises "in the name of Jesus of Nazareth. Hear ye the words of the Lord."

Boatman, to the shore! Return to your nets and your fishes until you hear the call of the Lord. Will you follow Him?

Oh! the beauty of God's earth. This loveliness gives one the fulness of peace and rest. A Japanese Christian viewing this part of God's garden the other day shouted, "Glory to God in the highest!" Shall Japan also own the beauty of holiness? Before the Sun of Righteousness will shine in His fulness and in His glory, there must first be conflicts that will try men's souls and men's faith. God or no God, is the question, and here center the forces of a severe struggle. Gird your loins![23]

The seminary building was completed on Septmber 18, 1891, at the cost of $7,416. A handsome brick structure with square tower, it had four recitation rooms, a chapel, "several other apartments" (small domiciles for personnel) and the Kelker Library with 3,269 volumes, of which 1,338 were in Japanese, the others being in English and German. On one wall hung "a suggestive picture of Kelker." The building stood next to the Ault Memorial Hall and old temple still used by Sendai Church. There were 119 students, 61 of whom were Christians. The new name of the school was changed to Tohoku Gakuin, known in English as North Japan College. It had received recognition from the Japanese government and was officially rated as an institution of higher learning. To get this it had been necessary to revise and extend the curriculum. "But official recognition does not interfere with our Christian intent for the school."[24]

Two articles for *The Missionary Guardian* depict Hoy's evangelistic trips. One described the babies crying while he was preaching and his singing to the children.

This is my favorite exercise with children. While we are singing, a crowd of street-venders, rickshaw men, errand boys and others may be seen gathering about the open front of the building. Singing always attracts a crowd. Now my Japanese assistant jumps before the crowd and preaches Jesus and His Love. We continue to hold our teaching while we lower our voices so that the preacher's words may be distinctly heard. The sermon is held in sight of the street, all the shoji (sliding doors) having been previously removed. As the services proceed a few men and women, too timid to enter for fear of the Buddhists, assemble on the outside and pay good heed. Sometimes they gain enough courage to enter and sit down."[25]

The other article described a trip to Miya five miles from Sendai to hold a service in the home of a physician whom Hoy "had led to Christ after a life of wine and bad women."

> Rickshaw men come and eagerly ask to take us. It pains one to see a strong man take the place of a horse. But by employing one of them you put rice into the mouths of a family of children. To run for rice! A great part of the world is full of anxious thoughts about what to eat. I often feel like walking rather than being pulled along by a human being, and yet a refusal might mean great pain for the little ones. Yes, I will ride, and may God bless the few pennies you earn, my trusty rickshaw man.
> What strength and endurance these men possess. One of them once took me 40 miles in about eight hours and seemed none the worse for his day's work. Some years ago, I took a long ride in Pennsylvania and my fine large horse broke down at the end of 35 miles. Here we find men pulling men in a little two wheeled carriage with the speed or endurance of an ordinary horse.
> The women, beasts of burdens they have become, are carrying large stones in wicker baskets on their backs. They drag their weary way to the riverside where, with a short upward thrust of one shoulder, they empty their baskets. Back and forth they go, resting now and then to suckle a crying infant. Again, the old struggle for a bowl of rice. The world must eat.[26]

For reasons not recorded the formal opening of the new institution was not held until the following year, on November 18, 1892. The gala event in the presence of the Governor of Miyagi Prefecture and the

Mayor of Sendai, which was scheduled for 2 p.m., but which didn't begin until 3 : 30, was rather fully reported in *The Messenger*. A portion of Hoy's address was included and is worth noting because it is the only one from his Japan years which remains.

> By faith in Jesus Christ as the Saviour of the world, and as the center and norm of the highest civilization possible to the world in general and to Japan in particular, and by prayer to God as the Creator, Upholder and Supreme Governor of the universe, were the foundations of this institution laid in the obscure work of our beginnings six years ago. Along with the seeds of human learning, we sought also to plant the infinitely more important truth of man's worth as created in the image of God.
>
> Thus we have built and thus we are determined to continue, in faith, in prayer, in communion with God, in service to Jesus Christ, in service to the Japanese. If we fail to do this, the best friends of this institution need not care how soon it perishes down to its foundation stone. When Christian voices cease to be heard and Christian influences to prevail in these halls, let the hand of destruction pull down every beam and every brick into the dust. Then let the hissing serpent come and make its home in the ruins and do its deadly work upon the hand that may so much as touch the last signs of a miserable failure.

There is no indication whether Hoy spoke in Japanese or in English, or in both, or through an interpreter. Oshikawa and Schneder gave addresses too, and Mayor Yendo "spoke in warm commendation of the school." Because of the limited capacity of the chapel, the students could not be present.[27]

The completion of the new seminary building marked a milestone for the Japan Mission of the German Reformed Church. Though its work in Japan was just twelve years old and its pioneer activity in Sendai only half as long, Sendai had been firmly established as its center with two growing schools, each of which was housed in splendid western-style buildings. Also, three houses had been provided for the missionaries who with the arrival of Miss Hollowell that fall numbered nine. It was uncertain whether Mrs. Moore's health would permit them to return from furlough. Although education had become the central thrust, the work of direct evangelism was expanding. The number of Christians was growing and the churches were becoming stronger, though the tempo had somewhat diminished. At age thirty-four Hoy was the senior missionary on the field and also the central figure. But new problems were emerging, and with them new testings.

Footnotes

1. Hoy letter to Board, Feb. 27, 1890.
2. Kelker letter to Hoy, Aug. 7, 1890.
3. *The Messenger*, June 19, 1890.
4. Kelker letter to Hoy, Mar. 26, 1890.
5. Hoy letter to Board, Mar. 18, 1890.
6. *Ibid.*, Mar. 20, 1890.
7. Schneder letter to Board, Jan. 16, 1890.
8. Hoy letter to Board, Aug. 33, 1890.
9. *The Messenger*, Apr. 23, 1891.
10. *Ibid.*, Oct. 30, 1890.

11. Hoy letter to Board, July 23, 1890.
12. *The Messenger*, July 23, 1890.
13. Hoy letter to Board, Aug. 23, 1890.
14. *Ibid.*, Feb. 1, 1889.
15. *The Messenger*, Oct. 30, 1890.
16. Hoy letter to Board, Sept. 20, 1890.
17. *Ibid.*, Dec. 30, 1890.
18. *The Messenger*, Feb. 12, 1891.
19. *Ibid.*, June 19, 1890.
20. Hoy letter to Board, April 8, 1891.
21. Mission Proceedings, Mar 12, 1891; Hoy letter to Board. May 2, 1891.
22. *The Messenger*, Mar. 26 and June 18, 1891.
23. Hoy letter to Board, Feb. 12, 1889 and April 1891; Mary letter, Dec. 29, 1890.
24. Hoy letter to Board, June 16, 1891 and Feb. 22, 1889; *Messenger* Nov. 5, 1890.
25. Hoy letter to Board, May 2, 1891.
26. *Ibid.*, June 6, 1891.
27. *Ibid.*, May 25, 1891.
28. *Ibid.*, June 6 and 28, 1891.
29. *Ibid.*, July 18, 1891.
30. *The Messenger*, June 28, 1891, Nov. 5 and Aug. 4, 1892.
31. *Missionary Guardian*, Sept. 1891.
32. *Ibid.*, Oct. 1891.
33. *The Messenger*, Feb. 9, 1893.

CHAPTER VII - BEGINNING OF DISSENSION

"I am weary of the misunderstandings." June 9, 1892.

With the promulgation of the Meiji Constiution in 1889 and the Imperial Rescript on Education the following year, Japanese nationalism and the Emperor system which informed it were firmly established. Military conscription had been instituted in 1873 and the basis for imperial expansionism was being laid. The euphoria for the West had diminished and reaction was growing, especially against the unequal treaties with the humiliating extraterritoriality which had been imposed by the western powers. The popular mood was changing, with Christianity, especially the Japanese Christians and the missionaries, the easiest and most immediate target of attack. The implication for Christian work were many, with the reactions against the West expressed both without and within the Christian fold. Outside reaction ranged from open hostility and subtle opposition to complete avoidance of any kind of relationship with Christianity, while within the Christian fold the nationalistic spirit often expressed itself in the reaction of Japanese church leaders against the missionaries and the Home Church.

Hoy had alluded in his writing to such difficulties, but the first time the problem emerged for him in a specific way was in the spring of 1892. Matsuda, the perennial problem student, was trying to get money from Moore in the U.S. for his own independent activities which included plans for an orphanage. To the Board Secretary Hoy wrote,

"If the Japanese Christians could get money from our Church at home without the official channels of the Mission and Board, our life here would be intolerable." In explaining the details involving Matsuda he added, "How far Brother Oshikawa encourages Mr. Matsuda I do not know." His next letter two weeks later was more candid.

> Will you tell me the precise nature of the agreement existing between the Board and Brother Oshikawa? What authority is lodged in him? Can you send us the contract? Tell us about every understanding you have with him. It may become necessary before long to define the relations between the Mission and Brother Oshikawa. Some of the native brethren, if not all, seem to have the idea that the Board appointed him as bishop of the Mission. Brother Oshikawa is a good man and it were far better for him and for us if he could be delivered from his Japanese friends who inspire in him perhaps a little too much personal ambition.[1]

Two months later, in acknowledging receipt of the Articles of Agreement between the Board and Oshikawa, which unfortunately has not been preserved, he reassured Secretary Callender that "present relations are pretty much as they ought to be. Brother Schneder and I have had some pretty plain talks with our native brethren and they seem disposed just now to honor our rights and privileges. We have the understanding that if they do not abide by these conditions it may become necessary for us to sever our relations. It's not likely that we will have any further trouble in the near future."[2] While Hoy championed Japanese ownership of the property and the leadership of the school by Oshikawa, there were obviously limits to the amount of Japanese control which he deemed best. Under the best circumstances, working out the most creative relationships between Japanese and missionary colleagues was a difficult venture, but the growing nationalism complicated the task considerably. There were also limits concerning how far Hoy would press and even to how outspoken he would be.

A far more candid informant of the mounting difficulties with the Japanese was Lizzie Poorbaugh who from the beginning had stubbornly resisted such attempts to completely control the Girls' School of which she was the principal. A year and a half after the founding of the school, and long before Hoy even hinted to such problems, she had written to the Board.

> The Japanese are so jealous of foreign influence that although they want foreign support very much, they also want to make it subservient to their own ends. They are also very fond of having authority. The Christians do not hesitate to tell us that the money we spend for missions in Japan is the Lord's money and not ours, and therefore ought to be spent according to the dictates of Japanese wisdom rather than according to ours. Without contributing anything to the school so far they have nevertheless tried hard to have things their way, and if they have any real authority in the school I am afraid it won't work well. I don't know what they will ask, but it is likely to be a good deal.
>
> If we give the Japanese equal rights in the school with ourselves we will scarcely be able to carry out our original designs. The Japanese who will have control will not be, I fear, for the most part Christian.[3]

Two and a half years later, in the fall of 1891 the problem became intense. Poorbaugh's correspondence is worth quoting at length not only because it throws much light on the complex problem but also because it reveals much about Oshikawa, who was becoming something of an enigma, and about Poorbaugh herself.

Oshikawa brought forth a plea to put the Girls School under Japanese management and I very much regret that action but thought it best to let him send his proposition to the Board, for if I assume an attitude of any sort in the matter, it will be the end of my connection with the school. I do not think Japanese men fitted to have the care of female education, and therefore cannot approve of doing so in our school. If they gain their point the influence of the foreign teachers will be reduced to a minimum and their effect wasted. In such a school I could not remain. If they do not gain their point they will probably ruin the school entirely by taking away our pupils. I consider that the one point upon which American women sympathize with Japanese women is the looseness of the marriage relation. During the vacation I had occasion to address to Mr. Oshikawa the strongest appeal I am capable of making to stand between one of our best girls and a marriage which is no marriage. The answer to my appeal informed me he was the negotiator of the marriage and he cooly told me I had "no need to worry" because he would be responsible for the morality of the matter and could not be musted. The man the girl is to marry is a brutish fellow, a deposed evangelist, who left his wife and children. If the girls are in the hands of native Japanese this is all we can expect. As for me I could not work under such direction.

Mr. Oshikawa will probably propose one thing which on the face may seem very possible, but experience teaches me that no Japanese can be bound by any treaty with a foreigner if he sees fit to be unbound, unless the foreigner can maintain with .... If I could attribute any other motive to Mr. Oshikawa than race jealousy I should be more ready perhaps to listen to his projects. He admits that the girls are well trained, that the work is efficient, and all who come in contact with the girls notice how different they are from other girls, but the Japanese can't endure that any civilizing process in their country should be directed by a foreigner.

A month later she continued.

I am waiting for an interview with Oshikawa which is hard to arrange. Our school is not the only one with such problems. All over the country the same demands are being made. In Sendai the boys' school is under Japanese control, and that makes it hard for us. I feel that to give the school over to the Japanese would be to convert it into a sort of literary kalaidescope or workshop for young Japanese men. Mr. Hoy remarked to me that we cannot succeed till we do give the Japanese a hand in the management, but I dispute his point. If by success we mean a large number of pupils it may be so. If we mean a large number trained in firm Christian principles, it may not be so. The complaint is that we don't inspire them with a love of their country. Again, no need of such teaching on the part of foreign teachers, as that principle is so deeply in their hearts that nothing can eradicate it. We acknowledge the beauty and righteousness of their gentleness and patriotism, but we urge them to hold to their gentle temper, purity, truth, faith, and high ideals of womanhood. To their patriotism we urge them to add love of God and service to his Kingdom.

The papers are full of adverse criticism of mission schools. To read them one would suppose the missionaries who came to Japan have come with the united purpose to denationalize and corrupt the land.

Japanese have told the girls it is not good to visit the foreign teachers or in any way be under their influence. Finding they could not come between us in that way, they tried ridicule and that too being unsuccessful denounced the school. True, Mr. Oshikawa says if it must be, I may be principal, but with a male board of trustees and all male teachers. That would be ridiculous.[4]

Two weeks later she confided.

Should my views influence the Board to see as I see, I'm altogether unwilling that a suspicion of the fact should ever reach the ears of the Japanese. For in that case I should be expelled from the school. That I, a Christian woman, should oppose the views of any non-Christian man in this Empire is, in Japanese judgment, all right. My Christian principles would receive the credit for it, but that I, a woman, should attempt to thwart a measure urged by Rev. Oshikawa is an entirely different matter. For that my unwomanly assumption of superior female excellence would be ascribed as the reason.[5]

The trouble spread when some of the students demanded the dismissal of a certain teacher and agitated against certain rules and requirements. Poorbaugh was convinced that behind it all was a teacher at the boys' school. She became so suspicious of Oshikawa, that she no longer trusted him. Finally the ringleader, Kotaira Koyuki, and others were expelled, for which Poorbaugh was much critcized by members of the Sendai Church. But Hoy and Schneder supported her, and Oshikawa promised that none of his teachers would do anything against the Girls' School thereafter. Yet Poorbaugh remained skeptical.

> They all, Mr. Oshikawa included, consider it highly right they should take control of the school out of foreign hands by fair means or foul. And to have any consideration or respect for the conscientious scruples in respect to the responsibility of foreigners who have been in the country less than ten years is a thing of which they neither have or wish to have any conception. Mr. Oshikawa speaks very grandly of the terrible responsibility resting upon him as head of the boys' school, but utterly ignores any of responsibility devolving on me in a similar position in the girls' school."

She went on to say that Emma was all broken up about it but that she was sure everything would come out all right. Yet in concluding she remarked, "the time for unbelievers to harm the Christian cause in Japan has passed, but the believers themselves seem determined to pull down what they have already shown themselves incapable of building up."[6] Although Hoy never referred to any of this, it could not have helped but influenced him because it happened just before the trouble with Matsuda. This led him to request the Board to clarify its relationship with Oshikawa.

Another recurrent problem with Oshikawa was his poor health, and even more so, that of his wife. During his summer in America it had been necessary for him to take an almost complete rest. Then a year later back in Sendai he had not been able to work from mid October until late February. At the same time Hoy's health was always uncertain and often incapacitating for brief times. It became increasingly obvious that his problem had not been caused by living in Japanese houses, as he had first assumed. It was not until early 1892, after he had been living in a western house for three years, that he identified his problem as asthma. His attacks were lasting as long as ten hours with much loss of sleep and laying him low for a couple of days each time. For several months he gave up preaching to save his limited energy for his teaching and other necessary duties. "This takes the starch out of a fellow," he had written to Callender. Finally the Mission insisted that he needed a change of climate, so in mid February he went to the somewhat milder Yokohama for three weeks where he described himself as "a very vigorous invalid."[7] Considering such limitations and the burdens they imposed, his accomplishments become even more remarkable.

The spring before the new seminary building was completed about 1000 volumes were received for its Rudolph Kelker Memorial Library. They were standard works of references in theology, science, philosophy, history, travel and exploration, poetry, fiction, general literature, pedagogics and other basic disciplines. The new school year opened with forty students and there were more scholarships from the Home Church than applicants.

Hoy added Sanskrit and French to his studies and informed Callender of his desire to study in Germany during his "missionary vacation" which would surely be granted in the next few years. "The Bible is the object of all my studies and nearly all my teaching. I feel more and more the necessity of the best means of systematic study of the Book that must receive increasing attention in Japan." He loved to study and once confided that one of the things he regretted most about his busy life was his sacrifice of scholarship. He generally took a book with him to read whenever he had to wait for something, which was not infrequent, especially on his week-end evangelistic trips.[8]

One such trip, which was fully reported in *The Guardian*, another church publication, is worth recording. He and Schneder had gone to Masuda, but the train broke down and was three hours late. Then they had to wait another three hours in an inn for their audience. "How do we spend our time while waiting? We usually take books with us!" The meeting which was well atended, even by some of the leading men of town, was the first Christian gathering ever held there. Ten years previously Oshikawa had been driven out of town.

I wish I could picture the scene of one of these evening lectures. How the people sit in circles around the braziers and smoke, now and then holding their hands over the few glowing coals ; how some of the school boys smile at the odd pronunciation of the stammering foreigners ; how a hireling of the Buddhists cries in dissenting tones the little monosyllables, 'No, No' ; how the wind comes in at the open sides of the house ; how the faces before you suggest fresh thoughts of the fulness and meaning of humanity, and how the touch of soul with soul and spirit with spirit, thrills you with the deepest sentiments. But you cannot look in upon us. Much less can I tell you the reality.

Come and see. The world is open to all.[9]

An account of a different kind of trip, published by the same journal, also deserves inclusion.

Though the fatigue of a walk of twenty miles might be excuse enough to retire early, my heart is so full that I must have another "chat" with you. As there was no regular engagement for me this Lord's Day, I strolled forth early this morning in search of something to do for the Master. Ten miles up through the hill country north of Sendai I passed in contemplative mood in full communion with the visible forms and invisible spirit of nature. The sun was painting the hills and the snow capped mountains in all the colors of the rainbow and of sentiment. Imagination aglow with the holy fire of the day peopled the autumn palaces of foliage with a million beings clothed on in poetry. The little hamlets among the hills spoke of the peace and retirement of the husbandman. Overhead a few clouds kept guard, scarcely moving in the lazy atmosphere. Earth felt secure in silence.

Soon the musical sounds of a brook tumbling down its rocky bed over little falls broke the deepening charm. I paused and leaned over the bridge and watched the living waters and listened to the waterwheel below. The old mill, the rice-hulling mill, creaked and thumped; the workmen sang a monotonous strain; the little ponies neighed with delight to be relieved of their burdens of new rice; little children dipped their feet into the brook and shouted at some dogs barking beyond the miller's house as the reflection of a large bird passed over the face of the brook; the frightened fishes darted hither and thither till their alarm was spent; a thousand thoughts arose out of the crystal fluid and danced merrily in the air, and I was dreaming of the dear old streams so familiar to my childhood. A Japanese came up to me and saluted me, and the realities of life drew me out of my revery. And the world is the richer for its streams and old mills.

At the end of my walk, up among the hills overlooking the snow regions of Yamagata, I stopped at a tea house and partook of some refreshments. After another long dream over the scenery before me, I prepared to set my face homeward. I now took out some tracts and distributed them among the guests and inmates of the tea house, adding a few words by way of explanation. For a distance of ten miles I saluted all travellers, lifted my hat, bowed and smiled, asked their destination and told mine, presented a tract, exhorted some, and passed on. In this way I reached more than two hundred souls today. Only one man refused to respond to my greeting. Some expressed a positive interest in Christ and asked my residence and permission to come and hear more. One man invited me to call and see him at his home. A poor old woman, sick and crippled, reclining on a rude cart drawn by her little grandson, had many questions to ask. Before I finished my conversation with her, tears of joy rolled down her cheeks. Her weary life was cheered by those words of interest in her welfare. When I passed on, I frequently turned and looked back, and as far as I could see the boy and old woman were still at the same place, and I doubt not that they read all the tract before moving on. The tract was on the redemption wrought in Jesus' blood. I would walk a hundred miles to make one poor old woman happy with the touch of human sympathy. And I verily believe that divine love has a response in her soul. God grant it.

When I reached home I was so tired I could hardly walk up the stairs leading to my study , but a drink of water, an orange, and an hour's nap, put me in fair condition again.

The experience of this Sabbath, so full and so varied, have taught me volumes. Preaching by the wayside touches on countless chords of human life, and the notes are not without the best characteristics of spiritual music.[10]

But there were hard realities to face and burdens painful to bear; one was financial and the other, the mounting tension with the Board. For Hoy the hardships of life in Japan were far outweighed by the troubles which ensued from the lethargy of the Home Church. A few months before the seminary building was completed, in one of his many pleas for funds, he had written, "I sometimes feel as if I were not worthy to be a missionary. I feel I have shown great weakness in our recent trials, but I could not well remain silent under those burdens which really belong to the Church at home. But if our cares have resulted in a better understanding of her duty on the part of the Church, all is well that ends well."[11] That summer he poured out his pent-up assessment of the Church to the Board Secretary in the tones of an Old Testament prophet.

> I will not work many years longer for a Church that refuses to be obedient to the plainest voice of God. We are doing our duty to the utmost and we have a God-given right to expect both Board and Church to stand by us. We have hardly enough courage left to make known our wants, for it is in vain to make any request. There is a terrible sin somewhere, or else there is no God. Don't you know that this lethargy of the Home Church hangs like a millstone around my neck.
> Now I understand why so many infidels say that the Church has

caused them to lose faith in God. Oh! the temptation you folks bring upon the world in general and upon me in particular is of the Devil. If people loved God or really believed in God and wished to follow Him, they could not neglect that larger and darker portion of the human race which is in the darkness of idolatry. I care not for doctrine. I would not fight two seconds for a catechism or a creed, but I believe in Christ as a personal Redeemer and I own the right of the heathen world to the love of the so-called Church of God. With the modern means of gathering information on Foreign Missions no minister is guiltless for this neglect. Oh! the hypocricy of the Ministry! I know some very bright young Japanese who went to America to study for the ministry, but who returned infidels, having stumbled at the mouth of Hell in the so-called Church of God. Love and Life and Practice. Pages on pages and volumes and volumes of theory and creed will never save the world, nothing but a downright self-sacrificing love fashioned after the sacrifice of Christ is going to avail. And the Japanese are beginning to see the hollowness of much of the church life in America, and even pray that Japan may have a more genuine religion of the Christ who did all he could for a sin-sick world.

I have witten and written, begged and begged, for five years. At the door of the Home Church I lie sick and faint as I see the terrible creature that is occupying pulpit and altar. A monster form of worldliness and selfiishness creeps in and out and leaves a slimy path upon which some seekers after God slip and fall into the modern Hell of unbelief. And the cries of agony and despair that go up to Heaven will bring down, God only knows what. According to Christ's own teaching, it will be more tolerable for the heathen at the judgment day than for the hypocritical Church.

Among the lost may be two classes, those in ignorance of Christ and those in neglect and disobedience of Him. Just now a poor, degraded, slovenly woman with a dead infant to bury comes for twenty cents to pay for the funeral rites at the temple of wooden gods. In the name of Christ, my wife gives the money as the last act of tender love to be done to the dead child. O God, how can thy people remain so blind and so listless in this work of bringing a sin-sick world to Jesus. These souls hang upon my conscience, and the sinful neglect of our Home Church also clouds my spirit.

Yours, I hardly know how to subscribe myself, for the pain and the gloom that is in me. Yours at the throne of grace for a sick Church and a dead world. Yours in the sight of sin and death.[12]

In November when the final payment on the seminary building was due, he wrote to ask the Board whether this meant he should add the $200 to $3,200 already owed him, which would be in addition to the $5,000 of his own money he had used. He quipped, "I am not afraid of extreme poverty, but should like to be prepared for it in a business like manner." Then he was incredulous to discover that the Board had sent out Miss Hollowell without providing for her salary. "The Board is ungallant to a young girl." It was three months before her first funds came and for the next half year they were irregular and late. "The poor girl is worried and it is too bad to put such a thing on a new and untried missionary, a hellish neglect of duty." He went on to compare the Reformed Church with the Southern Presbyterian. Though about the same size, the latter contributed about $100,000 annually to foreign missions and had more than 100 missionaries in Japan, China, Mexico, Greece and Africa. "The dumb idols will speak out against the Church. I pray I live long enough to speak face to face with the Church.¹³

Hoy's relationship with the Board increasingly became strained. The Board asked him several times to apologize, which he refused to do. In June 1892 he informed Callender that he was putting the Ault Memorial under a trust to be held by the Board.

> I am weary of the misunderstanding between myself and the Board and I now have made these arrangements whereby all my contributions amounting to $5,000 will be in full possession of the Board to hold and use as the Board may see fit for educational and religious purposes only.
> If I am in such bad repute with you all, it would be better for me to resign. I know I have faults regarded so by the Board , but I know also that these very faults so called have enabled me to do what few men have the courage to do. I love Tohoku Gakuin as Christ loved the world. These $5,000 were literally taken from Mrs. Hoy and my own life blood. I'm trying to make you see your duty as I see and feel mine. I cannot apologize. I am honest in this, not stubborn. If you wish me to do so, I must simply resign. And in one sense I dread ever going before the Home Church. If I ever speak to them it will be from my own convictions and experiences. I hold that you are all, in a measure, still undisciplined in the best matters pertaining to Foreign Missions, nor do I consider myself able to teach or guide you. Hence cometh my growing silence.¹⁴

The new school year had opened that spring with 170 students, with Hoy, who had just returned from recuperating in Yokohama, giving the address.

"I made some plain remarks on the social evil of Japan and charged the boys to be pure in mind, pure in spirit, and pure in body. They boast of their patriotism. Let them serve their country, their Emperor, and their God by being pure and by treating their Japanese sisters as vessels of holiness. I charged them with the sacred work of purifying Japan from an evil that is now threatening her very life. These earnest men want to put Japan on an equality with the foremost nations of the earth. Work for this end, but remember, your country will always be measured by the position you accord your women. Japan calls you to be living standards of sexual purity.[15]

Hoy himself was teaching about four hours a day, New Testament Exegesis, Greek, Philosophical Basis of Theism, Psychology and English. But he confessed, "I have been in this country six and a half years and I am thoroughly ashamed of my inability to acquire this tongue. Under existing circumstances I despair of ever learning Japanese thoroughly." In publishing Hoy's report, *The Messenger* added an editorial note explaining that Hoy was teaching and preaching in Japanese, that he had supervised the erection of all the buildings of the Mission in Sendai, and had been the treasurer of the Mission for four years.[16] *The Messenger* also reported that Oshikawa had opened the Industrial Home, a boarding school to help needy students to be partly self-supporting. Applicants were closely screened with respect to character and purpose, and of the thirty-three who were admitted, fifteen were Christian. The discipline was strict and the purpose was to "cultivate the spirit and habit of self-dependence and self-help in acquiring an education." The students expected to work two or three hours a day at jobs "which yield income", such as delivering newspapers, working as street vendors, caring for poultry, and other odd jobs. Their food was plain and their clothing cheap. Oshikawa was in sole control of the management of the Home and also personally responsible financially with no mission funds involved at all.[17]

In March 1892 the Toka Gakko was finally closed because of mounting opposition against its Christian orientation from within and without. Also there was increasing competition from the Second High School opened by the government in 1887. Almost from the beginning there had been dissension over its Christian program, and the financial support from the Japanese proved to be much less than had been expected. Finally in 1892, when the Bible courses were removed from the curriculum, the Christian teachers resigned and the Congregational Board decided it could no longer support such a school. The DeForests, however, remained in Sendai until their deaths two decades later, with Dr. DeForest becoming one of the most prominent foreigners in Japan.

The demise of this venture by the Congregationalists left Tohoku Gakuin the only Christian secondary school for boys in Sendai, and in the entire Tohoku there was only one other such school, Toogijuku, founded by the Methodists in 1873 in Hirosaki. But with this new challenge and unprecedented opportunities came new difficulties as the national mood continued to swing against the West and Christianity. Yet in 1892 the Baptists opened Shokei Girls' School under Miss Lavinia Meade, and the following year the Catholics started Shirayuri Gakuen for Girls under Sister Isaac Tuvache from France. It was not until 1897 that the first public school for girls was opened in Sendai.[18]

On July 25, 1892, a daughter, Gertrude Blanche, was born in Tokyo, "large, fat and healthy." Hoy made the trip from Sendai by bicycle later. In reporting the good news to the Board Secretary he also asked what the policy toward the Salvation Army should be, because one of the students of Tohoku Gakuin was trying to get a scholarship from General Booth in London. He also was grateful for two additional professors, a Mr. Kumagai and the Rev. Henry K. Miller. Both were recent graduates of Union Theological Seminary in New York City. Miller, also a graduate of Franklin and Marshall College, was designated as the "Sunday School Missionary" because that organization provided his full support. During his long career in the Tohoku he served with competence in a variety of ways, including intermittent teaching at both Tohoku and Miyagi Gakuin. He also served as the fourth president of the latter school from 1908-09. Upon arriving in Sendai he had lived with the Hoys, and in 1898 he married an Episcopal missionary, Sarah Sprague. With the addition of these two new teachers Hoy was not slow in advising the Board that new land and buildings would be neeeded for the Preparatory Department and the College.[19]

Mary Hoy worked through a trained helper known as a "Bible Woman," which was becoming the practice of many married missionary women. Yoshida Misao, daughter of that large Christian family outside Tokyo which had been baptized by Gring, began working for Mary in the fall of 1891 after leaving the Girls' School a year before she would have graduated. Though not a brilliant scholar she proved diligent and faithful and responsive to Mary's tutelage. She spent her mornings studying the Bible following an outline prepared by Mary, and in the afternoon she engaged in a variety of evangelistic activities, with Mary accompanying her as often as her other duties permitted. On Monday she went to Matsuda to hold a woman's meeting and teach knitting. On Tuesday she did home visitation. "She does not wait for an invitation to go to places, but goes out for a walk and with some polite excuse asks if she may enter the homes. As Japanese houses are so open, it is very easy to do this and Misao San has met with nothing but kindness so far. She delights in working among the poor. She has already gathered a number of Sunday school scholars from such visits." On Wednesday she went to the home of a Christian and read the Bible to a blind man whose wife was almost deaf. "The good man says they suit each other well. He is her ears and she is his eyes." On Thursday she went to the hospital to look after the work that Mrs. Moore had begun.

I think this is her happiest time of all the week. She has permission to visit all the rooms, but seldom finds time to go to all. In some rooms the patients shut their ears and mouths and will have nothing to do with her, in others they welcome her and are glad to listen and to receive the books and tracts. Not long ago she went to the door of a room in which there was just one woman. On asking permission to enter the woman said, "You can come in if you wish, but I do not care to listen to your talk. The new religion you are preaching can do nothimg for me". Misao San said, "I would like to tell you the story of Jesus." The woman answered, "You can talk if you wish but I am not bound to listen." Nothing daunted, my girl began and before she was through tears were rolling from the eyes of the sick woman, and when she offered to stop talking was told to go on. Then the woman added, "I hear that the Christians never care for their dead and do not visit their graves." Misao told her about the beautiful cemeteries we have in America, on hearing which the woman brightened up and said, "Well, if that is true, perhaps there is something in the Christian religion. Will you please come to see me again and tell me more.

Friday afternoon was spent teaching the Bible and knitting to some young girls at the Hoys' house. Saturday was her day of rest. Sunday was her busy day. In the morning she helped at Mrs. Schneder's Sunday School and in the afternoon at Mary's in Nagamachi, while in the evening she attended the Sendai Church. Mary concluded her report with the following example.

Misao noticed a poor woman in church who went and came several Sundays without speaking to anybody, so she made it her business to bid her welcome. The woman has seen a great deal of trouble. She was once quite well-off, but her husband became insane and his friends sold all the property. When he died she was left with four children and no home or money. One son is now old enough to teach school. He receives seven yen a month. This, with ten sen a day that she earns making tabi, must pay the rent and buy the food. She said she had worshipped at all the temples in Sendai but received no comfort from the gods. Finally she heard of the Christian religion and began going to church. Now she is sure she has found rest for her soul. We pay Misao six yen a month and she fully earns every sen of it.[20]

Thus, the work moved forward despite the difficult national mood and the dissensions it produced, for behind it all was a common Christian purpose which persevered.

Footnotes

1. Hoy letter to Board, Mar. 27 and Apr. 9, 1892.
2. *Ibid.*, June 9, 1892.
3. Poorbaugh letter to Board, Jan. 16, 1888.
4. *Ibid.*, Sept. 21 and Oct. 12, 1891.
5. *Ibid.*, Oct. 24, 1891.
6. *Ibid.*, Jan. 31, 1892.
7. Hoy letter to Board, Feb. 11, 1891, Feb. 10 and 24, 1892, Mission Proceedings, Jan. 18, 1892.
8. Hoy letter to Board, Apr. and May 14, 1891.
9. *Ibid.*, Nov. 1891 and *The Guardian*, Mar. 1892.
10. Hoy letter to Board, Nov. 15, 1891; *Missionary Guardian*, Feb. 1892.
11. *Ibid.*, May 25, 1891.
12. *Ibid.*, July 25, 1891.
13. *Ibid.*, Nov. 19 and 24, 1891.
14. *Ibid.*, June 9, 1892.
15. *Ibid.*, Mar. 30, 1892.
16. *The Messenger*, Aug. 4, 1892.
17. *Ibid.*, Mar. 2, 1892.
18. C. DeForest, *Evolution of a Missionary*, p. 180 f.
19. Hoy letter to Board, July 27, 1892; Poorbaugh letter to Board, July 1, 1892.
20. Mary letter to Board, Ap. 25, 1892.

Chapter VIII - BEGINNING OF RECONCILIATION

"We have all learned a good lesson. The Father, in his infinite love and pity, does not allow His weak children to dwell long apart." Sept. 29, 1894.

Tohoku Gakuin prided itself from the beginning on its high moral standards and strict discipline, in comparison to the rather lax government schools. Hoy's writings often refer to the lewdness and drunkedness of such students. In one essay he described the ribald parties of the government college where "they fool around with unchaste singing girls who will dance half naked, sometimes stark naked, before these lewd fellows and then pair off with them for the baser rites of Venus." One of the purposes of the Gakuin was to raise up a new type of Japanese through the "education of the whole man to be developed Godward." In his "1892 Report on Tohoku Gakuin," Hoy elaborated on this rationale.

Tohoku Gakuin has no uncertain work to do, and she turns like an inspired virgin to the defined life and love of the future, hoping only for the fulfillment of the heavenly aspirations God has implanted in her noble breast. With her doors swung open to the admission of the enthusiastic boys of the Church of Christ in Japan, the sounds that issue from the consecrated halls also bring influence to bear upon boys not yet in Christ, so that these come hungry, yet leave rejoicing in both new knowledge of the things and mysteries of this earth and wisdom in the things that pertain unto the spiritual life that now is.

Let the God-given and God-prospered work continue in its normal progress and we shall fear no future, however dark and unpromising in financial matters.

Yet courses in religion and chapel attendance were not compulsory, "and on the whole this has been good... By years of experience we have found it best to make instruction in the Bible optional, excepting for candidates for the ministry. Voluntary study of the Bible is worth much more among ten students than compulsory instruction among a hundred."[2]

Hoy, along with Schneder, remained highly appreciative and supportive of Oshikawa despite the difficulties that had occurred. In his 1892 Annual Report Hoy wrote as Vice President,

Oshikawa is the right man in the right job. His influence over young men is second to none in the Church in whose interest Tohoku Gakuin has been established. His unselfish devotion to the welfare and advancement of our students have made him a very useful man indeed. The students love him as their father. In the enlargement and improvement of the school during the past year, he has done an important part.

For *The Messenger* Hoy characterized Oshikawa's speeches to the students. "He speaks of the needs of Japan and what kind of men must meet these wants and work out the problems of this developing country. He always finds his solution, his ends and ideals, in the Lord Jesus Christ. Men made in the image of the God-man must shape

Japan." In the same article he reported that the widow Kami was working as a nurse in a military family, living "within sight of my study, and has agreed to sit for her photograph."[3]

In December 1892 Hoy proposed to the Board the inauguration of the Tohoku Gakuin Self-Denial Fund, "to promote my own personal pattern of giving for the home people to follow, which is but a natural outcome of my mission and work in Japan." His plan, to be presented through *The Messenger*, called for pledges of one dollar a year for ten years. "A smoker by smokng one cigar less a week can give one dollar a year." In his accompanying appeal he set forth succinctly the evolving purpose of the school.

> Together with the purpose of training up young men for the Gospel ministry, we have come in the Providence of God, to enlarge the scope of our institution. We have now a Preparatory Department of three years, a College of four years, and a Seminary of three years. For the theological students alone it is necessary here as in America to provide a liberal culture. With the same amount of teaching we can extend the privileges of our institution to young men not studying for the ministry. We need also a liberally educated laity to witness the best life and thought of Christianity in the various walks of life. The young church here needs an institution in which the different department of human learning shall be made to center in one rational system of truth in Christ Jesus, in which the human mind shall be lifted beyond the concrete and the utilitarian and in which mental discipline shall look to the perfection of man's character in his threefold relations to Nature, to Man, and to God.[4]

He insisted that "Tohoku Gakuin is heel and heart of our evangelistic work." During its seven years of ministry the number of organized churches had increased from one to twelve, Sunday Schools from three to thirty, baptized members from 149 to 1800, and contributions from ¥18 to ¥3023. For him this justified the educational policy of the Board which was ratified at General Synod in 1890. In an article for *The Guardian* he described the school as "an institution of liberal Christian culture." Of its 170 students, half were Christian, 52 were studying for the ministry. Of these 20 were regularly engaged in Sunday School work and 9 at preaching stations. Furthermore, all the teachers were Christian.[5]

The Board, however, was not receptive to Hoy's special appeal because it was planning a campaign to pay off its debt, to which Hoy promptly donated $20. Yet he persisted with his project, reporting in April that he had already secured pledges in Sendai which would raise $3,000 in five years. Oshikawa and several of the professors were giving one-tenth of their salaries. He warned that if the Board decided against his efforts for the school he would not return on furlough but become independent. "If need be, I will undertake, with what help I can get here, to go ahead single-handed. When I went through that former long, untold struggle to get the material interests of the Gakuin under way, I was a thousand-fold happier than I am now in trying to get help from home."[6] Instead of authorizing this special appeal for the school, the Board incorporated Hoy's idea of self-denial offerings into a larger campaign for liquidation of its debt, which proved to be most successful.

Precisely at this time Hoy found himself in another unhappy misunderstanding with the Board. The occasion was a mix-up over the payment for books for the Kelker Library which Hoy was ordering from Scribners. He had instructed the treasurer, Lemberger, to pay the bills and charge his own personal account for the amount in excess of the designated book allowance. According to Hoy, Lemberger had not made any deductions from his account, and then without notifying him had chided him both by mail and before the Board for being financially irresponsible. This led to an unpleasant exchange of letters between the two men, with each insisting he had acted correctly. This led Hoy to resolve, "I shall hereafter ask no favors of you or the Board. With all my severe labors for the cause of the Board and with all my sacrifices I have usually met nothing but questionable treatment. But I care very little any more what men may say or fuss about. I serve God and him only."[7] The problem continued to fester for several months. Finally Hoy insisted to Callender, the Board secretary,

> I want you to decide once for all whether I am worthy of your further confidence. If I have your confidence it must be henceforth perfectly understood that no individual member of the Board, nor even the Board itself, is to chide me for what I can prove I am not guilty of. If I no longer have your confidence, let me hand in my resignation and cut off this farce. These frequent resolutions and letters of censure must be stopped. I had rather draw a rickshaw and be self-supporting than to submit any longer to these ill-advised letters and resolutions the Board thrusts upon me.[8]

At the same time, Hoy had taken the Board to task for its discriminatory salary scale which was $700 for single women, $800 for single men, and $1200 for married couples. He argued that women should be paid the same as men, and that married couples should receive $1400, but he gave no reasons for this latter figure. In words typical of him he concluded, "I had rather serve elsewhere for less, than continue longer in your service under the present unfair and unbusiness-like scale of salaries. I have been faithful and I demand justice." The Board agreed and revised the scale accordingly.[9] Then there was the problem of the Hoys medical bills for 1892 which had exceeded the $100 annual allowance. Mary had gone to Tokyo to have her baby because there was no longer a foreign doctor in Sendai and Hoy had gone to Yokohama for his asthma. Hoy argued that none of this was his fault. "To put my family under the care of a Japanese physician requires a little more grace than I happen to possess. Why does a married missionary with a growing family get only the amount of a single missionary ? That you should refuse to pay the expenses of last summer's confinement without even a word of notice or explanation is beyond my comprehension."[10]

All of this was extremely distressing to Hoy and his wife. To clear the air and set the record straight he poured out his heart to Callender in a poignant epistle.

> That I am always in a state of friction with the Board is a matter of pain to me. This is not to my taste. When I was a youth at home and in public school and then at Mercersburg and Lancaster, and

today in my relations with the Japanese brethren and with the Mission and Foreign Community—I say in all these relations—I was and am at peace. But ever since April 8, 1886, when I first penned the words, "By the grace of God we shall soon have two schools in Sendai, one for girls and one for boys," and when good old Dr. Johnston took me severely to task for my sanguine words about educational work, there has been nothing but a succession of clashings with the Board. Of course, I might have avoided all this, if I had from the first been indifferent to the best interests of God's Kingdom in Japan and taken the sense of the Board as final, but in a love of souls as deep and sincere and comprehensive as that which the Board has ever reiterated, I took my choice after a most profoundly prayerful meditation on things here and after numerous consultations with Brother Oshikawa made in earnest prayer and with many tears. I thus took my choice between an easygoing silent concession to the mistaken judgment of the Board and the alternative of taking up heavy burdens to be borne perhaps for a life-time. In an immoral way, as a faithless and indolent servant of Jesus Christ and of the Japanese, I might have said, and I even was tempted to say, "All right, the Board has said so and so I am no longer responsible for what my judgment dictates here on the field nor for what Brother Oshikawa and other experienced Japanese Christians tell me." Then it might have been smooth sailing between the Board and myself. I might have refused to listen to Brother Oshikawa's pleading just three days after my arrival in Japan and might have remained in Tokyo, and Sendai with its large and promising work would have remained practically unknown to you and there would have been no Tohoku Gakuin to fight about.

And even today I might with more excuse perhaps, than at the inception of the Mission's work in Sendai say, "All right, the Board has enough of me and my aggressive plans. I am no longer responsible for what experience and most tangible success have taught me and what Brother Oshikawa and many other experienced Japanese ministers and educators tell me. I might plead such excuse and purchase a guilty peace with the Board, and spend the remainder of my days in an easygoing round of duties in the lecture room. But, Oh! The love of souls of Japan, and of God, does not let me rest here. God has given me a rich experience and I am resolved to go on as resolutely as ever. With the moral and spiritual support and inspiration of such men as Oshikawa and Schneder I can go on. The future calls. O Lord, I consecrate unto Thee in the upbuilding of the Tohoku Gakuin, that this institution, which Thou hast so richly blessed hitherto, may become a still greater temple of eternal truth and life for the salvation of Japan.[11]

Two months later he wrote a very brief official letter to the Board.

I hereby tender an unreserved apology for all things said and done in the past that may have given you collectively or individually pain. My motives were always good and my convictions remain unchanged, but as the Secretary repeatedly says, I am giving you pain. I must express my regret that any unguarded words or deeds should have hurt your feelings.

One of my grievances is removed by the frank acknowledgement of the Secretary that you made a serious mistake in the matter of the single missionary salaries and that you seek to remedy the same. God help us all.[12]

On July 1, 1892, three months after the trouble in the Girls School had climaxed Lizzie Poorbaugh informed Secretary Callender that she and Emma were resigning effective the following summer. She cited three reasons. The events of the past year had confirmed her growing realization that she was not the right person for the job and that her work was finished because her experience with Oshikawa had made her distrustful of even the best Japanese men. She added, "Hoy and Schneder, too, are harrassed on every side by the cunning and deceit of the natives. For myself, during the past two years, I've been on the edge of insanity or the grave." Also she had not been able to acquire the Japanese language sufficiently to function even in a minimal way and "thus being literally deaf and dumb among them, for me to have charge of the moral training of the girls year after year is simply a caricature of mission work." Lastly, "in a few short years my duty to Kittie will require my return." Her conclusion was that "the school is run by men determined to pervert its Christian aims."[13] All attempts to persuade the Poorbaughs, who were much esteemed, to reconsider proved futile.

Anti-Christian feeling was flaring up in incidents. According to Mary,

> The devil is still very active in Japan. As my Bible woman was returning from Sunday School a number of boys threw stones at her, several hit her on the back, others spit at her. At one of our Sunday Schools below Sendai a number of boys were punished by their school teacher for attending Sunday School and the number of students has greatly decreased.[14]

140

At its January 1893 meeting the Japan Mission moved that since those Japanese who held property in behalf of foreigners were liable to public attack, it would be "better that our land owners, some of whom are in public positions, should be directly responsible to a Board here." A year later Hoy wrote in *The Messenger*, "On the part of Buddhists and the lower classes opposition has never been stronger. Public preaching is much disturbed, and I and others have been stoned. Missionaries and Christians have probably never been scoffed at and jeered so much as now. But probably also the Christians have never been so earnest and decided in their faith as now."[15]

No record has been found of Hoy's appraisal of the Sino-Japanese War which broke out on August 1st that year. Schneder, however, like many of his colleagues, firmly supported Japan and interpreted Japan's eventual victory as promoting "Christian" civilization and eventually Christianity, because Japan was deemed the most modernized country in the Far East.[16]

In Hoy's writing a recurrent theme, typical of his missionary generation, was the "evil of idolatry" which was held responsible for many of the personal and social ills of Japan. It was in this sense that the word "heathen," whose original meaning was "pagan" or "those who do not believe in the One God" became perjorative. Idols were the concrete manifestation of everything which Christians opposed. Freedom from idolatry was the way to salvation. On one occasion Hoy described renting a room for a Sunday School and asking for the idols to be taken out "because they were so obscene he didn't want the ladies to see them," obviously a reference to phallic worship. About his four-year-old son he wrote, "Our little Willie is quite a missionary already. He has a deep-seated fear and horror of idols, and frequently asks people whether they pray to idols. He says, "You mustn't pray to idols. You must pray to Jesus." Would to God that we could all preach from the heart as he does."[17] This was one of the emphases, though by no means a dominant one, in the promotion of the work back home. Mary contributed to *The Missionary Guardian* an article entitled "Fox Worship in Japan," which still may be the best description in English of the history and rationale of the huge Takekoma Shrine at Iwanuma south of Sendai. Her own appraisal of this fertility cult, whose rituals offer protection and success, was reserved for the last. "As the people are becoming more civilized, the old ways are dying out and fox worship is becoming less popular. The old people say that the power of the god is becoming weak because the powers of men are becoming stronger. The Lord grant that the day may soon come when fox worship and all other forms of idolatry may be wiped out of the land.[18]" But for Reformed Church missionaries salvation was not from some kind of hell for heathen after death, which was an image they never used, but rather from futile religion and suffering in this life without Christian faith and hope.

In the spring of 1893 the Board, at the urging of Hoy's father and friends, informed Hoy that he could take his furlough, but Hoy replied that without a replacement he could not leave. One reason was that he was planning, at Moore's suggestion, to publish a non-denominational bi-monthly journal, *The Japan Evangelist*, in October.[19] As editor he gathered together reports of the activities of the various missions throughout Japan and articles of excellent quality on Japanese culture and religion. Each issue of about sixty pages featured a Japanese Christian or missionary leader, complete with a full page photograph, and also a photogravure of some aspect of life in Japan. Some articles were so substantial that they were continued in subsequent issues. There were also poems about Japan from a Christian perspective. Writers included not only missionaries who were quite well-informed but also other foreigners as well as many Japanese. The journal was published by Yokohama Seisha Bunsha, and the agent in America was Rev. C.L. Ferner of Mt. Pleasant, Pa. The yearly subscription was $1.00 or ¥2. The quality of everything including the paper was excellent, which led the Board Secretary to comment in recommending it to the churches, "Its get-up is really superior and will compare well with our American periodicals, and in instances not a few, it excells, witnessing to the progress in the arts in that oriental land."[20] In the fall of 1896 it became a monthly with more than twenty denominations represented. It continued until 1927 when it became *The Japan Christian Quarterly*. It comprises a valuable resource, not only on the missionary movement but also on certain aspects of Japan during that period. This is especially true of the early issues, now collectors' items, for they cover a time when materials on Japan in English were few.

  In the spring of 1894 it was finally decided that Mrs. Hoy and the children would go to America and that William would follow within the year. The Hoys decided to pay the expenses for Yoshida San, Mrs. Hoy's Bible Woman, to go along. She would do much to promote the work back home and also be of much help with the children, of whom there were now three, Mabel Ruth having been born on October 8, 1893. But again there was trouble with Treasurer Lemberger who wrongly assumed that Hoy intended the Board to pay for Yoshida's travel.[21] Carlisle was chosen as their place of residence because it was near Mary's family, as well as near Harrisburg. Hoy also asked the Board for advice about his personal finances, confiding that he had been giving everything to the work, over $5,000 to date, but that his best friends and his own "meditation" had convinced him to make some provision for his family and the education of his children. He added that he didn't like insurance.[22] Hoy also became increasingly unhappy that *The Japan Evangelist* wasn't being better received back home, especially in his own denomination. "Why is it that most of my best encouragement comes from beyond my own church. I don't understand." Thus one of Mary's chief tasks upon returning was to promote subscriptions, and for a while it seemed as if the journal would flounder.[23] In explaining why he couldn't accompany his family, Hoy again vented his dissatisfactions with the Board and 'Home Church.'

> In all my relations with either the Board or the Church I shall ever act as best I know how, but I am slave to no one. Even a missionary, despised and derided though he may be, has freedom of conscience. This I will sell to no Board, neither will I limit it to the confines of a sinfully conservative Church. Christ and His Kingdom are infinitely more to me than Board or Church which are mere accidents. I cannot run away from Japan at a moment's notice. I have served the Board and Church only too faithfully, and for what

purpose ? To have my most earnest and sacred letters laughed at in meetings of the Board. You will have noticed that my letters have been few for about a year. I will never write much hereafter excepting as I speak to a larger constituency.[24]

He added, "I fear my strong convictions and blunt way of putting them will make me anything but a welcome visitor." Two days later he assured Callender that he did not wish to leave the Reformed Church, but that it was necessary for the Board to know where he stood, since "I have been asking for bread for more than eight years and have gotten scarcely a stone."[25]

Just when he was at that low ebb, with his family back in Pennsylvania, Hoy's situation at the Gakuin and his relationship with Oshikawa went through a painful crisis. The records concerning the problem are few and can be quoted in their entirety to speak for themselves. Schneder, the Mission Secretary, alluded to the difficulty in the following explanation appended to the minutes of the June 9th Mission Meeting which he sent to Callender.

> Brother Hoy feels himself aggrieved by the state of his relations to the school, and also by a change in the curriculum that has been proposed. I do not know whether he will make any communication on the subject by this mail. I think he takes a very extreme view of the matter, and perhaps after fuller consideration, he will think differently. It would be a calamity if he should lose interest in the school.[26]

The minutes of the September 15th meeting record that Hoy had resigned the presidency of the Board of Trustees as well as his positions as vice-president, treasurer, professor, and librarian. Yet Hoy promised his good will and active interest in the school. The Mission voted, "Resolved that sometime in the future the way may open again for Brother Hoy to renew his invaluable labors for the school." In an accompanying letter Schneder explained,

> For more than a year Brother Hoy and Brother Oshikawa have had difficulty in understanding each other and working together harmoniously. The difficulty has affected others more or less. On the 10th instant, Brother Oshikawa presented his resignation as president of the school. Upon this Brother Hoy presented again his own resignation which he had offered last November. After all possible effort had been made to prevent the break, it was finally thought best to accept Brother Hoy's resignation. Little or nothing of an unseemly character took place and Christian grace was always larger than our differences.[27]

After his resignation Hoy contributed ¥200 to the school and a similar amount to Oshikawa's Industrial Home. Finally, the October 10th Mission Proceedings noted that Hoy had withdrawn his resignation. Hoy referred to this crisis only twice. In his letter to the Board on June 6th he wrote that *The Japan Evangelist was* "a means of forgetting the frictions and annoyances incident to my peculiar relations to Tohoku Gakuin." Then on September 29th, he wrote,

You will rejoice with us in the fact that by the prevailing grace of God there has come to pass a perfect understanding between Rev. Oshikawa and myself. I go back to the Tohoku Gakuin. Thank God! His love still dwells in our hearts. We look to Him to guide us in the future. My Japanese friends, as well as our Mission, have been very kind to me in this severe ordeal. We have all learned a good lesson. The Father in His infinite love and pity does not allow His weak children to dwell long apart. Christ today seems much more real to me than ever before. Yes, I go back to my old, old love —the Tohoku Gakuin.

Promoting *The Japan Evangelist* occupied Hoy increasingly. "Its origin lies in the desire to make myself more widely useful in the cause of Christ, to bring the East and West closer together, and to give more information about Japan and the work to the people of the Church."[28] When he learned that his critics back home were saying that he was neglecting his regular work in its behalf, he was indignant. "No one on the field has ever hinted such an untrue and unkind thing. Such unfounded accusations are cruel. God knows the work is hard enough without such letters."[29] He wondered why all of the members of the Mission Board did not subscribe, especially his retired friend, Kelker. Mary had written personal letters to six hundred pastors, but received replies from only fifty. Hoy suggested that an effort should be organized to put the journal in every Reformed Church home. To Callender he pleaded, "I have suffered so many disappointments in the past. Make this magazine the grandest success of my life, for Christ's sake, for Japan and for the Reformed Church."[30] He gave up all hope of taking his furlough and asked the Board to send his family back by Christmas. "I am a very lonely man. My house is empty and quiet. So is my heart."³¹ He had been in Japan almost nine years and was clearly in need of a change. It was also obviously imperative for Hoy and the Board members to meet personally to get to know each other better and improve their relationships. In November, just before Hoy suddenly left on furlough, he sent another passionate letter asking for more confidence, sympathy and love. "I must say in all frankness that my best work has always been along those lines where the Board most misunderstood me." He reminded Callender that he had "virtually made bricks without straw in the material development of the Gakuin," and that he was "the largest donor to your mission plant in Japan, now upwards of $6,000. At the same time have I been slothful in teaching and preaching? Great God! Has it come to this that I must defend myself like a common criminal?" He concluded by saying that in the past three months his journal was doing very well. It was "financially on its feet" and he was receiving very appreciative letters from a variety of people in different foreign countries.³²

Tohoku Gakuin gave Hoy a festive farewell on December 1st at Bairin, a well-known Sendai restaurant, with addresses by Oshikawa, Schneder, and student representatives. Sendai Church held a farewell service with Rev. Hashimoto, who had been Hoy's language teacher, in charge. Words of appreciation for his many achievements and sacrificial service were many, and duly reported by *The Messenger* to the people back home. Hoy sailed on December 7th on the Empress of India and reached his family on Christmas Day. The Sendai pioneer, age 37, had returned home where there was much work to do. Just before leaving he had written to the Board that he would "not study in Germany but devote that money and time to the Lord's immediate work in Tohoku Gakuin."[33]

Callender, however, warned Hoy not to speak about mission policy, which condition Hoy said he could not conscientiously agree to.[34] Hoy spent much of his time speaking in the churches where he was most cordially received. In thirteen months he travelled about 33,000 miles and gave about 400 addresses to over 100,000 people. There is no way to judge the financial results, but they surely were not insignificant. The Philadelphia Classis at its spring meeting donated $3,000, while the church in Alexandria assumed the support of Miss Yoshida.[35] Yet within a few months Hoy was eager to return to Sendai. From Ohio he wrote to the Board Secretary, "I am mentally very uneasy these days. I feel that I ought to go back to Japan. The developments of Tohoku Gakuin will largely depend upon me and my own personal contributions. We are only losing time, money and opportunity here in America."[36]

On May 15, 1895, Kaneko Kinzo, Hoy's Japanese friend from his student days, died in Lancaster after a brief hospitalization just before he was scheduled to return to Japan to teach Old Testament at Tohoku Gakuin. He had graduated from Franklin and Marshall College in 1891 and from the Seminary in 1894 where he had remained for another year. In college he had become known as George, and in an 1888 publication entitled *The Flame* his name appears among the sophomore students with the poignant comment, "Among us but not one of us."

During his eleven years in Lancaster he had become much loved and respected for his gentle character and steadfast faith, especially in his calm acceptance of his rather sudden suffering and approaching death from a chronic pulmonary disorder at age twenty-nine. His funeral in the overflowing chapel of the seminary was a moving testimony to the power of the Christian faith in its worldwide mission. Both Hoy and Apple delivered short sermons. Hoy's unfortunately has not been preserved, but Apple's was printed in *The Messenger* along with brief tributes from an unidentified classmate and a Japanese pastor in Lehighton. Burial was in the college plot in Lancaster Cemetery. But this extraordinary young Japanese Christian had captured the hearts of many. The terrible loss sustained by the work in Sendai presented a challenge which brought forth a most remarkable response from the church people. The Kaneko Memorial Fund was soon initiated by the Philadelphia Classis with the Lancaster and Mercersburg Classes participating. The Foreign Mission Board gave its official approval, although at first it had reservations about such an extra financial solicitation, fearing it would interfere with the regular giving. The Fund was duly designated for the seminary in Sendai. Within a year it reached $15,000 and eventually totalled about $25,000. This represented an amazing sum of money, almost equal to the annual budget of the Mission Board at that time.[37] That spring Franklin and Marshall College awarded Oshikawa an honorary Doctor of Divinity degree, which, however, he declined.[38]

Early in 1896 Hoy received a letter from Oshikawa asking for financial help. The Industrial Home had lost some cows worth ¥1,000 and Oshikawa was in debt. Hoy referred his request to the Board with the comment that he himself was in no position personally to help. Then just before leaving for Japan in June he learned that Oshikawa was in deeper debt. "His expenditures are far in excess of his receipts. He took on a lot of men this spring in spite of his debt. He is a grand teacher and preacher but a poor financer. If there were nothing but success, Brother Oshikawa would not consult with any of us. A grand financial smash-up of the Industrial Home will for a time greatly affect Tohoku Gakuin. It will mean the President's financial dishonor."[39]

The relationship between Hoy and the Board was much improved, as their correspondence in the years ahead would reveal. Among the materials covering Hoy's seventeen-month furlough only one item related to policy can be found and that exchange posed no difficulty. The Board had asked Hoy about the proportion of time missionaries should give to teaching and to evangelistic work. Hoy's characteristic reply was, "I do not see the propriety of making two questions out of one work. All our teaching is evangelism and our evangelism helps our school work."[40] Hoy also strongly urged the Board Secretary to visit Japan.

The Hoys left Mifflinburg on June 15, 1896, with much concern for Hoy's aged father as well as for his sister who was "mentally worse than before." With them went Yoshida San and little David Schneder Hoy who had been born in Lancaster on November 1st the year before. They arrived at Sendai station on July 8th at 2 a.m. with missionaries and Japanese there to welcome them.[41]

TWELVE PIECES OF SILVER

[There dwells in an humble hut a certain poor widow of Japan. Her husband died a few years ago. She lives in the barest penury, and is burdened by a drunken son. The shadows of poverty and desolation might well be driven into her heart; yet she is patient. A few years ago she found the Lord and Saviour Jasus Christ, and now through all the clouds of her domestic troubles she hears the voice of the Father. Day by day she goes on in the path of Christian joy, content if haply she may find enough to eat. Though poor and abused by her son, she never loses her faith in her Master. Her love of God and of souls in its glow reminds one of the 'Apostolic days." This godly woman longs for the spread of the gospel throughout the length and breadth of her dear country. Hearing of our school projects and desiring to aid the cause of raising up young men for God's work among her people, she comes forward quietly and makes an offering of twelve old Japanese silver quarters, which she had held in private and secret treasure for many years.]

In a low and lonely dwelling, where no touch of wealth has been,
Where the wrinkled hand of sorrow in its palsied form is seen,
Lives a widow of this city, toils a woman for her meat,
Well contented if her larder gives the smallest fish to eat.

Pain of poverty is doubled when her fallen, hardened son,
Homeward staggers from his revels, as his wasted day is done;
Proud and thoughtless, mean and idle, worthless as the wine he
                                                   drinks,
To the level of his choosing by a natural law he sinks.

Hot, his poisoned blood consumeth, with an angry, fiery flame,
The fair structure of affection, leaving but its blackened frame;
What to him are love and duty? They are as an empty name;
Mother—God—Home—Heaven—Spirit—but he knows not whence
                                                                         he came.

In the anguish of her spirit, in the bitterness of night,
Thoughts come stinging; hopes lie shattered by the *andon's** sickly
                                                                             light.
Dreams of food and raiment fading, sense of shame is running deep
To the fountain of all weeping, melting off her hold on sleep.

Wild and weird the shadows creeping, fast the fitful phantoms
                                                                           fleeting;
Visions through the dimness sweeping,—out of nothing comes no
                                                                           greeting;
O the burden of these moments! O her loneliness of grief!
Is for her no respite ready? Is there none to give relief?

Yet a little while she lingers in this weary round of care,
Times are hard and men are harder, and her burden she must bear,
Toiling long and waiting longer, tired of unequal strife,
Faltering in the growing struggle to preserve her simple life.

Night is night and yields to morning and the blessedness of day,
O the glory of the dawning and the splendor of the day!
Idol-worship is forsaken for the Dayspring from on high,
Peaceful coming of the Master, gentle footsteps falling nigh!

She the heavy laden widow, she the weary and the meek,
She for whom domestic trials wrought their lines upon her cheek,

With her suffering and her sorrow, kneeling at the Healer's feet,
Hears command of restoration, listens to evangel sweet.

Hers, in full and gracious measure, is the promise of the Lord ;
Font of hidden gladness springing till the Spirit is outpoured ;
Grace receiving, sins forgiven, and for her all things made new,
Out of error into wisdom, from the false into the true !

Like seraphic anthems swelling full around the Father's throne,
Songs of hope and adoration from her heart and voice alone,
Through her asking and her getting, through her loving and her
yearning,
By abiding inspiration into psalms of life are turning.

Now her newer life is budding, even in her evening hour,
Seed of grace in soil of sorrow, yielding finest fruit and flower.
Active service for the Master, who for her redemption wrought,
In the fullness of her gladness is her daily end and thought.

But her strength is soon exhausted ; pain the strongest soul can bind ;
Scenes of things she prayed and hoped for, half unfinished glide
behind.
White and ready stands the harvest ; what the reaping where none
reap ?
Mightier hands than hers are folded, listless as in careless sleep.

While the holy work grows dearer, helpless drops her willing hand ;
But her grateful mind is hopeful for the people of her land.
What can she in will or purpose for the coming kingdom do ?
What is praying without doing ? What the giving of a *bu* ?†

Soon she brings her household treasure, all the family chest doth hold,

But one dozen silver pieces, each a silver *bu* of old.
Small and simple is her giving, yet what truth it comprehends!
Tis the praying and the doing, tis the giving Christ commends.

"These are mine, and these I offer, though their value is not much;
They are old—my husband owned them—and I give them now as
                                                                                               such.
Multiplied by richer treasure from the hands that well can share,
Let them be for training reapers for God's harvest far and fair."

Deep as depths of willing spirit, shines her love of souls within:
Bright as suns are, pure as faith-star, breaking through the clouds of
                                                                                               sin,
Far and farther gleams its radiance, like the beacon lights of old,
Till the story of her giving to my countrymen is told.

Parents, children, men and women, learn the lesson she has taught,
Many hundredfold increasing, see the offering she has brought,
In the treasury of the Saviour, swells into a goodly sum—
Sacred money is sure leaven—Father, let Thy Kingdom come.

Hers the living, hers the giving, in the fruitage of the Word,—
Grapes from grapes and figs from figs,—full life which cometh from
                                                                                               the Lord.
Flesh is flesh and spirit spirit: born of God, the kindred mind,
In the season of its promise, blossoms after its own kind.

                William E. Hoy
                February, 1894. THE JAPAN EVANGELIST.

* (andon=lantern) † (bu=coin)

Footnotes

1. Hoy letter to Board, Nov. 20, 1892.
2. *Ibid.*, Nov. 24 and 26, 1892.
3. *The Messenger*, Feb. 23, 1893.
4. Hoy letter to Board, Dec. 5, 1892 and Feb. 7, 1893.
5. *Ibid.*, Feb. 13, 1893; *The Guardian*, Mar. 1893.
6. Hoy letter to Board, Apr. 25, 1893.
7. *Ibid.*, Nov. 25, 1892.
8. *Ibid.*, Feb. 3, 1893.
9. *Ibid.*, Jan. 23, 1893.
10. *Ibid.*, Mar. 6, 1893.
11. *Ibid.*, Feb. 13, 1893.
12. *Ibid.*, Apr. 25, 1893.
13. Poorbaugh letter to Board, July 1 and Aug. 24, 1892.
14. Mary letter to Board, Jan. 6, 1893.
15. *The Messenger*, May 3, 1894.
16. Mensendiek, A Man for His Times, P. 43-44.
17. Hoy letter to Board, Nov. 27, 1891, Feb. 24, 1892, Feb. 21, 1894.
18. *Guardian*, Mar. 1892.
18. *Guardian*, Feb. 1894.
19. Hoy letter to Board, Nov. 20, 1892 and Apr. 25, 1893.
20. *The Messenger*, Dec. 7, 1893, Hoy letter to Board, Sept. 1, 1893, Apr. 4, 1894.
21. Hoy letter to Board, Mar. 1, 1894, Aug. 19, and, Nov. 27, 1894.
22. *Ibid.*, Apr. 30, 1894.
23. *Ibid.*, Feb. 21 and Aug. 19, 1894.
24. *Ibid.*, Apr. 8, 1894.
25. *Ibid.*, Apr. 18, 1894.
26. Mission Proceedings, June 9, 1894.

27. *Ibid.*, Sept. 15, 1894.
28. Hoy letter to Board, June 6, 1894.
29. *Ibid.*, Aug. 19, 1894.
30. *Ibid.*, July 23 and Aug. 20, 1894.
31. *Ibid.*, July 23, 1894.
32. *Ibid.*, Nov. 27, 1894, Dec. 7, 1895.
33. *The Messenger*, Jan. 3 and 17, 1895.
34. Hoy letter to Board, Feb. 25, 1895.
35. *Ibid.*, May 17, 1895; Mar. 1896.
36. *Ibid.*, Apr. 23, 1895.
37. *The Messenger*, May 30, June 6, 18, 1895; June 11, 1896. Franklin and Marshall College Obituary VI, p. 246.
38. *The Messenger*, Sept. 5, 1895.
39. Hoy letter to Board, Mar. and June 6, 1896.
40. *Ibid.*, Feb. 8, 1895.
41. *Ibid.*, Mar. 1895; *Messenger*, June 1896.

Chapter IX - THE END OF A BEGINNING

"In helping Japan, forget not China." Sendai, Nov. 2, 1896

The matter of gravest concern to Hoy upon his return to Sendai in the summer of 1896 was the problem of Oshikawa in general and the Industrial Home in particular. A year before the Japan Mission had appointed Schneder and Moore to "confer with Oshikawa concerning his relations with the work of the Tohoku Gakuin and of the Mission in general." By way of explanation Schneder had written to the Board,

> Brother Oshikawa's earnest longing for the general advancement of Christianity in Japan has led him to give a considerable portion of his time and strength to work outside of our immediate bounds. He is a man of such unusual power that he should not be prevented from throwing the weight of his influence into the general current. Yet to prevent him from perhaps doing this to such an extent as to injure our work here, we thought it well to have a conference with him about the matter.[1]

Schneder subsequently reported that "concerning his relations to Tohoku Gakuin and the work of the Mission, Oshikawa showed willingness to acquiesce, as far as possible, in all the desires of the Mission."[2]

When Hoy returned, the more immediate problem was Oshikawa's indebtedness on the Industrial Home which had reached ¥2,000, "simply enormous for a Japanese." In addition to his loss of the cows he had been exceeding his income by ¥100 monthly. Oshikawa asked Hoy to loan him the money, but Hoy refused. Yet Hoy continued to be most appreciative of Oshikawa, especially with his preaching ability. "Whence has this man his power? From a living faith! The other Sunday he delivered a most searching sermon on Christ having come to save sinners. Few men can equal that sermon."³ In November Hoy reported to Callender that the land of the Industrial Home next to Moore's house would be sold and that it should be bought for Tohoku Gakuin with $2500 from the Kaneko Fund.⁴ The crisis was finally settled the following March when Oshikawa agreed to transfer the property of the Industrial Home into the hands of the Japan Mission which accepted full financial responsibility, with Oshikawa as superintendent and and the Rev. S.S. Snyder, who had arrived in 1894, as treasurer.⁵ Hoy concluded, "The whole Mission is a harmonious unit in all things."

Meanwhile trouble was brewing within the Miyagi Classis of the Union Church. In 1894 a movement had begun to put the evangelistic work completely under Japanese control. After two years of difficulty the Japan Mission had resolved that the work should remain completely under the management of the Mission with Japanese representation. The Classis then had threatened to withdraw from the cooperative work and organize its own independent work. But nothing happened until a year later when the attempt was made to get at least one of the seven missions of the Union Church to agree to the Japanese proposal, which Oshikawa was promoting. But all of the missions stood firm. Robert E. Speer, Secretary of the Presbyterian Foreign Mission Board, and one of the most noted mission leaders of his day, had told the Union Council that even if the missions in Japan agreed, the boards at home "would not sustain any arrangement that would deprive the missionaries of voice and vote in the management of work for which the boards and the churches at home hold them responsible." To Secretary Callender, Hoy wrote, "After eleven years of experience I would not for a moment conscientiously put any department of our work completely under Japanese control. Our recent experience with Mr. Oshikawa, and he controls all his Japanese brethren, has made us more cautions than ever." Hoy went on to report that he had told Oshikawa that he could not oppose Mission and Board policy and still receive his salary from the Board through the Mission. This is the first time that Hoy does not refer to his colleague as "Brother Oshikawa." Also a few of the theological students had told Hoy that they would never work for the Mission. Hoy had replied that he would close the school and the missionaries would do the preaching. This had silenced them. "We must be bold and firm to do the right where selfish ambitions run wild with good common sense. They will come to see that we are their best friends."[6] For Hoy, who from the beginning had championed the priority of the Japanese, such opposition was a grievous burden. "I cannot tell you how weary I am of this ungodly friction. The most painful part of this affair is the unscrupulous attacks that are made on me as the storm center of this Miyagi Classis." An evangelist had written letters against Hoy, but Hoy had not responded in defence. "It was a surprise to them that a man could be defamed without a desire to retaliate, and some of these men actually owe their best start in life, materially speaking, to my early struggles."[7] While a disruptive crisis was averted, the unrest persisted. Almost a year later Hoy wrote,

> The men who have caused us so much trouble in our evangelistic work seem to be coming to their senses. A committee appointed by the Classis and consisting of Rev. Oshikawa, chairman, and three of our Tohoku Gakuin faculty, and one elder, drew up a letter to be sent to all the preaching places. In this document they reflected on the Mission in general and on me in particular. They intimated that as we refuse to do as they wished we lacked the spirit of Christ, and did not strive to promote the Gospel of salvation. It also contained the statement that the Mission is a nuisance. In private Oshikawa says we do not represent the Church at home, that the Japanese evangelists have as much right to dispose of our money as our Mission has. The letter, however, has not been sent yet, and it likely will not be. Better sense may prevail. It is absurd to think that the four most prominent Japanese men in the Tohoku Gakuin should rise up to oppose our methods of evangelistic work because we do not give them the control. These men must come to their senses or leave our work, or else we shall have to go out. I believe they will soon see in full the foolish stand they have taken.[8]

The trouble in the Classis was paralleled in Tohoku Gakuin by a proposal in the fall of 1897 that the Collegiate Department be made into a government school and placed under complete Japanese control. Hoy rejected this approach as "useless." The missionaries had become firmly convinced that government support of Christian schools would mean their end as Christian institutions because the Ministry of Education was hostile toward Christianity and intent upon destroying mission schools. The Reverend Christopher Noss, who came to Japan in 1895 as a missionary of the Reformed Church to begin his long career by teaching at Tohoku Gakuin, commented in an article for *The Messenger*, "In Japan the most determined enemy of Christianity is the Education Department. It is generally surmised that the Christian teachers in the government schools of Sendai do not associate with other Christians because they dare not."[9] To the Board Secretary, Hoy wrote, "If the Japanese church is to have Christian schools, I believe the missionaries must show the highest example of purpose, faith and perseverance in their development, in their growth along humble lines at first."[10] The benefits from the government, financial and otherwise, would be great, particularly full recognition and exemption of students from military conscription which was causing students to transfer to the privileged government schools. But the cost of such advantages was deemed too high. Better to be under-privileged and Christian.

It was not surprising when Oshikawa requested a two-year leave effective April 1, 1898, "to do evangelism throughout the Empire." It was agreed that he would retain the presidency but with his salary reduced by half. Before moving to Tokyo Oshikawa "wanted an inferior man appointed to take his place at a large salary, but the constitution provided that the Vice-President, a member of the Mission, fill the place of the President when the latter is absent." Hoy's comment was that "Oshikawa regards Tohoku Gakuin as too narrow a sphere for him. We do not expect much service from him, but we think this is the best way to satisfy him. The next two years will no doubt settle matters permanently one way or the other."[11]

Soon after returning from furlough Mary made an amazing revelation to the Board Secretary.

> Mr. Hoy says I may tell you what I wanted you to know before we left your home. Almost six years ago when our Willie was six weeks old and I was quite sick, there was a call one night between eleven and twelve o'clock. The call said the American mail was at the door. I was asleep and did not hear it. Mr. Hoy went down and when he opened the front door three masked men with drawn swords met him and demanded money. Just the day before he had received $4,000 for the new school building. He had nothing to defend himself with and if he had showed any resistance they would have cut him down, so he opened the safe while they stood over him. After they left Mr. Hoy sat as if dazed until morning. Then fearing to tell me in my weak condition he hid it from me. Then he did something I think very few men would do. He was so in love with the work and so much afraid that the Board would not give any more money for a school that he made up his mind to give it all back out of his salary. So he shut it up in his heart and said nothing. But the strain brought on asthma and the debt is still a great burden he is carrying so bravely. I feel that the church should know it, for it was not his fault, and I believe the good people in the homeland would not allow him to struggle on if they knew all.[12]

Mary surmised correctly. The Board reimbursed Hoy completely, even including the six-year interest on the money. Hoy's subsequent account was printed in *The Messenger* and a Fund for the Relief of Rev. Hoy was inaugurated. Hoy's own account is worth recording,

> In October, 1890, one day late at night, I heard the familiar call "Yubin" Mail, at the front door. As usual, without a thought of danger, I went to the door. There stood three masked men, each with the deadly Japanese sword thrust into close proximity with my head and breast. They demanded access to the Mission safe. Refusal must mean death and even obedience might incur the same fate. Nervous as I naturally would be under such circumstances, it took me sometime to work the safe conbination. During this ordeal I expected to be cut down any moment. After the door was opened the robbers soon helped themselves to the ¥7,000, partly building fund and partly Mission funds. The men left without doing me any harm. Then, there I sat for hours before the safe. Words fail me to describe my feelings. For years I had toiled so hard and scarificed so much for our school and now in a moment all hope was gone! What would the Mission say? What would the Board be able to do? What effect would this loss have upon the Church at home? And so on. At last I cried out, "O Lord, put the burden on me. The work must not suffer. I will bear the burden! Thus for nearly seven years I have labored on and it has not been without its blessing, As my wife, several dear friends, and now the Board assure me that it is not right for me to go on alone in this matter, I reluctantly give these facts.

Yet he cautioned Callender about publicizing the incident in fear that it would hurt the cause with people saying that the Japanese could not be trusted. In order to prevent such a reaction he assured the Board

Secretary that he would gladly continue to bear the burden alone.[13]

A Yokohama newspaper, *The Hong Kong Telegraph*, however, in reporting the incident in its January 4, 1898 issue, criticized Hoy as irresponsible and lacking in common sense. By not reporting it to the police, who surely would have caught the thieves, he had let them go free to repeat their crime, and because of the risk, not only of burglary but also of fire, he had been derelict in not keeping such a large sum of money in the bank. Yet it also commended him for being able to repay such a large debt out of his small salary.

With the return of Hoy, the Schneders, who had been in Japan for nearly nine years, went on furlough. Earlier that year the Moores had moved to Tokyo and Miller to Yamagata. The missionary staff of Tohoku Gakuin, whose enrollment in the fall of 1896 was 154, consisted of Hoy, Noss and Snyder. Hoy taught eighteen hours a week, with his week-ends free from Friday noon through Monday for evangelistic work. In Nakamura he had "a peaceful meeting with about 400 non-Christians, in contrast with the meeting five years earlier which was disrupted when Rev. Yoshida of the Sendai Church had been chased down the street by a man yelling, "Kill him." The pastor had been saved by a man who had rushed out of his house to pull him inside where he had spent the night. Eventually that man and his whole family became Christians.[14] Hoy also preached the sermon at the tenth anniversary of the founding of Miyagi Gakuin, and this sermon together with others was printed and given to the members of the prefectural government. His special address at that occasion on Female Education was also well received and eventually published at the request of the public officials.[15] Another longer evangelistic trip in October was to Fukushima, Wakamatsu, and Sukagawa, much of it by rickshaw. One meeting had 600 in attendance. The account of another trip which appeared in *The Messenger* is worth quoting.

> About one month ago I went forth upon a pedestrian evangelistic trip in company with Rev. Yoshida. It was our aim to visit people in their homes, and bring the Gospel to them in a most direct way. With Bibles and tracts in our knapsacks, and "the holy hope of youth" in our hearts, we began a week's most earnest work. The first evening we held a lecture meeting. This was well attended and a good deal of interest was manifested. The next day we visited farmers and talked with them about Jesus. In the evening a man who was deeply impressed, threw open his large house and invited the neighbors to come in. We had a pleasant social gathering first and afterwards a good religious meeting. I feel confident much good was done then and there.
>
> A man who was to receive baptism came more than six miles to see us and to meet us. But he would not consent to being baptized there. We must come to his village and he and his whole household would be baptized in the presence of all the villagers. So early the next morning we went to his house. At three o'clock that morning the earnest old man had sent out a youth on horse back to call the people of the neighboring hamlets to the Christian meeting at his house. The simple joy and zeal of this old man was, I think, an inspiration to Bro. Yoshida and myself in our sermons. In the presence of this early congregation I baptized the three couples of that household, grandfather and wife, son and wife, and grandson and his promised bride. It was an impressive scene and we tried to press home upon our audience the beautiful spirit of it all.

Thus we went from village to village, from house to house, bringing the word of God, and receiving many more invitations to preach in private houses than we could accept. It was a matter of deep regret to be compelled to refuse the request of a man who walked some twenty miles to invite us to his village to preach. We consoled the disappointed man by assuring him that we would visit his village and house some time in the fall. And go we will.

In one of the villages the people threw open a large school building. Here again, a herald was sent forth on horseback to ask the people to come in, and they did come in, some six hundred of them, men, women and children. It was my first experience of preaching in a Japanese school house, the more gratifying when one considers the almost universal opposition of the schools of Japan to Christ. And we were invited to come again. In this village we were entertained by a man and wife who are not yet Christians. Their genuine spirit of hospitality was encouraging. The man carried water and heated the bath for us, and the woman prepared a good Japanese meal. At bedtime we held prayers with them, and then they did all in their power to make us comfortable for the night.

This evangelistic trip was made in the heat of summer. The fleas were at their worst. One night I had sixty-three poisonous bites, but I learned to sleep through them all. During our whole trip we did not receive a single rude or unkind word, or notice any act of hostility. Since my return I have received a number of kind letters from those honest-hearted people. A careful estimate seems to point out that seven-eights of the people of Japan live in the country, in villages and towns. Oh, what a field of immortal souls. I long to go to them with the simplicity of the Gospel. Pray for them.[16]

On February 13, 1897, the Nagamachi Church, which grew out of the Sunday School Mary Hoy had started six years previously, was dedicated. The Hoys had bought the lot and Japanese house for $350, including repairs, and the remembered tradition of the church claims that their gift was to commemorate their tenth wedding anniversary. Of the humble beginnings of this church, which is now one of the strongest in Sendai, Hoy wrote, "This town is a stronghold of one of the foulest forms of worship known to idolatry. The house contained a shrine of such a nature that I may not describe it. If we can do nothing else besides turning the one hundred children away from these abominable shrines, it will be enough."[17] That month Sendai had its biggest earthquake in sixty years. The Tohoku Gakuin buildings were damaged, while at the Girls' School two students panicked and jumped out of the second floor window. One girl broke both legs and the other sustained internal injuries. "An earthquake is no fun. Mabel wants to go to America where there are no earthquakes." In the same letter Hoy revealed that Mary was conducting kindergarten for their three oldest children together with eight other foreign children. Also Paul Gerhard was living with them, having just arrived in January to begin his long career as the first teacher of English at Tohoku Gakuin.[18] On September 28th Charles McCauley Hoy was born; the oldest of the five children had just turned seven. To Callender Hoy wrote, "Willie is learning to read and write. In fact, he has written some ten or twelve letters to his cousins and aunts in America. Gertrude, Mable, and David are growing finely. David is the autocrat of the household."[19]

That summer the Sendai Christian community was struck by a scandal when the principal of the Girls' School, a Mr. Saiki, was found to be ¥300 short on his accounts. He promptly resigned and was also expelled from the Sendai Church where he had been a respected elder, and eventually he went to jail. Painful as it was for all concerned, Hoy added, "The Buddhists will make capital out of this affair."[20] Two poignant comments on different subjects should be added. About himself Hoy lamented, "My busy life compels me to sacrifice scholarship, and to be a scholar was once a burning desire of mine." About the growth of Christianity in Japan, he observed, "Our work goes on slow but sure, but I do not look for any phenomenal progress in my life time. The Japanese heart is slow to turn to the living God."[21] Such realism stood out in vivid contrast to the prevailing idealistic optimism of many missionaries like Schneder who thought that Japan was becoming a Christian country, because Japanese religion was seen to be in decline and some Japanese in high positions were becoming Christians. Furthermore the advance of Western civilization was seen as promoting Christianity, and the hope was often expressed that by the middle of the twentieth century Japan would become a Christian nation and even the agent for the salvation of East Asia. Some even saw Japan's military expansion overseas in such terms, beginning with the Sino-Japanese War of 1894-95. Unlike Schneder, Hoy wrote no articles about such subjects. Yet his comments, though few, were cautious and often critical. This, of course, was in complete accordance with his own personal character and integrity. Also there was no place in him for any kind of nationalism which was at the expense of others. His was a Christian internationalism firmly rooted in the Kingdom of God which transcends place and time.

Hoy first mentioned China in a letter to Secretary Callender dated November 2, 1896. "In helping Japan, forget not China. Were I a younger man, I should go to the more destitute, and this plea of age may be an unholy one." The General Synod of the Reformed Church at its meeting in Dayton that May, at which Hoy had been present, had voted to start a mission in China. Hoy had been asked to go, but had refused. This call, however, had struck him deeply, and with his worsening asthma it increasingly seemed a providential answer to his plight. By the spring of 1898 it became imperative for him to have a complete change of climate, so the Japan Mission arranged for him to take a three-month vacation to China. Immediately upon arriving in Shanghai in early April he was completely relieved of his suffering. Instead of just resting there, he began inquiring among senior missionaries about a needy area for new missionary outreach. The prominent veteran, Dr. Muirhead of the London Missionary Society, strongly urged Hunan which was hostile to foreigners and where Christian work had just begun. Thereupon, Hoy went by steamer up the Yangtse 650 miles to Hankow to confer with the revered Dr. Griffith John of the London Missionary Society about starting work in the neighboring province. But before he left he had seen and heard enough to write to Callender that he was ready to be sent. "I offer myself to China. I cannot get rid of the idea that God is calling me here. The people in the Home Church have no conception of the abject poverty of millions of Chinese and no idea of the degrading superstitions prevailing in this land. It is not possible for me to keep quiet. I must urge our people to go to work and I am willing to lead the way." In another letter he candidly admitted, "Compared with Japan as a place of residence, China is exceedingly repulsive to me, but in the Lord's work, one must forget all these things at once."[22]

Back home the problem was, as always, insufficient funds to proceed without delay, as well as reservations about starting another mission. Schneder had also at first questioned the wisdom of such a new venture from the standpoint of the Board's limited finances and the growing needs of the Japan Mission, but Hoy had argued, "Not less of Japan but more of China." Hoy proposed using the $5,000 he had received in reimbursement for the robbery to buy a house on Tung Ting Lake and going in the fall of 1899, with his family following later.[23] When a writer to *The Messenger* questioned sending a family into hostile Hunan when they could work in comparatively safe Japan, Hoy answered in the traditional missionary spirit. "The missionary force is made up of sterner stuff than to shrink from possible danger when they are convinced God called them."[24] To promote the cause Hoy wrote eighteen graphic articles dated from April 13th to December 11th for *The Messenger* entitled "Shall We Go Forward?" Of the socioreligious situation he observed, "Those who praise 'the beautiful religions of China' can never be the true friend of woman. Confucianism has made the life of women a burning hell on earth." Then on a similar note he wrote, "What truth God may have once allowed to be faintly revealed in Buddhism, is, to my mind, lost in human darkness. Buddha's doctrine of woman fills my soul with horror; my heart sickens at it."[25] For him the imperative was clear. "The call to China is the strongest spiritual experience of my life. The sin, the poverty, the superstitions of the great mass of people in China appealed to my heart. On my return to Japan, the far prettier scenery and the far cleaner habits of the people caused me to shudder at what might be before us if we were to go to China."[26]

Secretary Callender, however, held up Hoy's twelfth article in which Hoy defended the sending of a family. In insisting that the article be published, Hoy also took the Secretary to task for writing to Schneder about his "running away from an unfinished work in Japan" and then asking Schneder not to tell him. "I object to such secret proceedings. Do my critics work and sacrifice and give while they criticize?"[27] Amidst the hardships of another winter in Sendai when his asthma was always worse, he pleaded with the Board to let him go even without all the money deemed necessary. "Do not hesitate sending me to China. Appoint me on faith. I am willing to go on faith. Others have gone to China on faith. I know I am weak, and so I simply put my trust in God. I am not afraid to go without the means in sight. I have seen how God rewards faith."[28] The Japan Mission at its March meeting went on record that Hoy could not remain in Sendai another winter, and that if the Board didn't open work in China, Hoy should either be stationed further south in Japan or be appointed as "financial agent in the Home Church." Subsequently an invitation came from the Dutch Reformed Church to locate in Nagasaki.[29] Noss expressed the sentiment of the Mission aptly when he quipped, "Our Mission without Mr. Hoy in Sendai would be like Hamlet with Hamlet left out."[30]

Finally in September Hoy received a cable from the Board that he could go to China as soon as possible. In anticipation of this move he had in June turned over *The Japan Evangelist* to two Baptist missionaries in Tokyo. This journal had become rather successful, for when he had stopped publication in October 1897 he had received so many encouraging letters that he had resumed it again the following January.[31] He had also presented to the Mission the deed to the Nagamachi Church property "to be held in trust for the Board," because the "unequal treaties" had been revised, with the Japanese government allowing foreigners to hold property.[32] Hoy's action represented a change in his original insistence that property be given to the Japanese, undoubtedly reflecting his sobering experience of recent years. In accepting Hoy's resignation the Japan Mission passed the following tribute.

> Resolved that we hereby testify to Mr. Hoy's zeal and fidelity in service, in spite of much suffering and many hindrances, while associated with us.
> Resolved that appreciating the difficulties of the new work upon which he has entered, we commend him and his self-sacrificing wife and their young children to the care and direction of our Lord, praying that the loss sustained by the Japan Mission through the withdrawal of this family may redound to the greater advantage of our Church's new Mission in China.[33]

This marked a turning point in the twenty year history of the Japan Mission. While Jairus and Annie Moore remained the senior veterans, they were back in Tokyo after brief periods of service in Yamagata and

Sendai. Except for the Schneders, the other nine members of the Mission were all more recent additions. With Hoy's departure Schneder became the senior missionary in Sendai, and also in a sense the leader of the Mission, since its center was in Sendai. Furthermore, with the resignation of Oshikawa in 1900 the full responsibility for Tohoku Gakuin passed into his able hands. Hoy and Schneder had worked well together, though the initiative had largely been Hoy's. The two men shared the same basic purpose though their approaches were often different. Their varying personalities complemented each other superbly. Hoy had been more aggressive but had come to believe that his work in Japan was largely accomplished. In his 1898 Annual Report to the Mission Board he had written, "In this new purpose of going to China, I am not unmindful of the continued claims of Japan. But from what I have seen, heard, and learned, I firmly believe that I can better serve the cause of Christ, for the remainder of my life, by starting new work in China, than by remaining in Japan." The Japan Mission was blessed by outstanding persons, beginning with the Moores and Schneders, then the Misses Hollowell and Zurfluh, the Millers, Snyders, and Nosses, and finally Gerhard.

Hoy was given a most cordial send-off in the way for which the Japanese were becoming well-known. His own words describe it best.

> These years in Japan have been full of blessing, toil, and love. Sendai holds much that is dear to my heart. It has been a hard fight; it is a stern conflict even now, to hold myself true to the lines of duty toward China. You will never know what this change involves for

me. The Lord calls and I dare not delay. The sympathy and the helpfulness of the members of our Japan Mission, of the missionary community of Sendai, and of other missionary friends throughout Japan, as well as of our Japanese Christian brethren, have been an unfailing source of strength. Without this touch of heart to heart, I should have fallen by the way-side long before reaching the shores of China. I can never forget the last prayer meeting of the Sendai missionary community that I attended just two days before I started. There were seven denominations represented ; and yet their prayers and expressions of love were undivided. They were one, as Christ would have them be. To respond to them was the hardest task of my life. Oh ! the depth of Christian brotherhood ! When shall the whole world be thus bound together ?

Of the farewell meeting in the Tohoku Gakuin, I presume others will write. You will, however, allow one reference here. The student who spoke as the representative of the theological classes gave this serious charge : Go fight the enemies of the Lord. We send you forth to the battle of our God, as a bride buckles the sword on her young hero husband and sends him on the the war. Be strong and fight the enemies of the Lord.' It was a pleasure to have Japanese friends, evangelists, former students meet me at the stations along the railroad, to say farewell and speak a kindly word of cheer and sympathy. The meeting at Kanda Church, Tokio, was an exceedingly helpful one. My first two Japanese friends, Rev. Oshikawa and Rev. Yoshida, were there ; so also was Rev. H. Shimanuki, my first pupil in Japan. At the Kanda meeting it was said that as I had always identified myself with the Japanese in Christian purpose and sympathy, I was, therefore, also representing the Japanese Church as missionary to China. A collection of more than two yen was given me for a chapel in China. Upon receiving this I simply broke down. The last sight of Japan, as we sailed away from Nagasaki and headed for Shanghai, brought a deep pang of pain. As I turned my watch back one hour to adjust it to local time, I thought this, 'Thus I turn back my course of life fourteen years and start again at the beginning of things.'[34]

The July 1909 issue of *The Japan Evangelist* featured a full page portrait of Hoy together with a long article by his colleague, Christopher Noss, who was then professor of theology at Tohoku Gakuin. After a brief biographical sketch and description of Hoy's pioneer missionary accomplishments, Noss concluded with the following tribute:

> Mr. Hoy's character defies characterization. He is trustful as a child, yet when it comes to business there is not a shrewder man of affairs to be found among missionaries. We have seen him rebuke a haughty Japanese professor for his "ungodly pride." We have seen him stand up alone and plead the cause of the erring when all others had yielded to despair. He is genial and sociable, frank and candid. He also has a prodigious capacity to keep a secret when he deems it his duty to bear a burden alone. He is a man of sudden and powerful impulse, but a man of rock withal. For his impulses are rooted in the love of Christ and kept within bounds by a spirit of sincere and fervent prayer and a scrupulous regard for the rights of his associates to whom he never denies the liberty he claims for himself. His acts are generally startling, but seldom mistaken. A born missionary leader, long may he live to bless Japan.

In just fourteen years the miracle of the loaves and fishes had been re-enacted. Two schools had been established and expanded. Property had been bought and three school buildings had been erected. The missionaries had been provided proper housing. Sunday Schools and churches had been started. The Mission of the Reformed Church had been firmly established in Sendai and was reaching out into the Tohoku. The Mission Board at home was firmly behind the policy with combined education and evangelism. The people in the 'Home Church' were awakening to the needs outside their parochial world. In pursuit of these aims the Hoys had given lavishly. Out of their salary of approximately $18,000 received during those years, they had used more than half for the work.

GO

William E. Hoy
Sendai, August 1899

O Lord ! we know thy will, and yet
    Unmoved we stand, and lose the day ;
We hear Thy call, but soon forget
    The curse is on us if we stay.
Our deepest feelings rise and fall,
    And hearts of stone are stone once more.
Our own short day is all in all,
    Our wills we hide a buried store.

O Lord! we hear; we, ill at ease,
    Shed frantic tears, and try by fits
With deedless plans our Lord to please,
    While each his friend exhorting sits.
The years are lost, our place of strength
    Goes with the sense of slothful shame.
A myriad souls, dead, lost, at length
    Upbraid our empty place and name.

O Lord! we hear out of the night
    Far China's voice, her one deep cry;
Ungirding we strip off our might,
    And listless on our couches lie.
Our dreams take on the form of hell,
    And souls that cried to us for aid
Curse from the places where they fell,
    "The fires we suffer you have made."

O Lord! we hear, our hearts are thine,
    For love is over all the earth;
Our wills are thine to make divine,
    When self is new in spiritual birth.
In consecrated hope we rise
    To do Thy will among all men,
To show all kings and teach the wise
    That Christ is more than sword or pen.

O Lord! we hear, and our long years
    Of wasted will and wasteful mood,
That shout our losses in our ears,

Would still beget their devil's brood.
But, Thou, O Lord! commandest, GO,
And go we will where Thou dost lead.
Let promise unto action grow,
And love be love in life and deed.

O Lord! we hear, 'tis holy toil
That in Thy vineyard Thou dost ask,
Dost bid the wealth of idols spoil,
And tear from Falsehood every mask.
We bring ourselves, we offer all,
In love of Jesus do we yield
Perfect obedience to Thy Call,
To reap in China's harvest field.

Footnotes

1. Mission Proceedings, June 15, 1895.
2. *Ibid.*, June 17, 1896.
3. Hoy letter to Board, Aug. 15 and Sept. 28, 1896.
4. *Ibid.*, Nov. 21, 1896.
5. *Ibid.*, Mar. 3, 1897; Mission Proceedings, Mar. 4, 1897.
6. Hoy letter to Board, May 1, 1897.
7. *Ibid.*, July 31, 1897.
8. *Ibid.*, May 19, 1897.
9. *The Messenger*, Feb. 25, 1897.
10. Hoy letter to Board, Nov. 6, 1897.
11. *Ibid.*, Nov. 6, 1897; Mission Proceedings, Nov. 16, 1897.
12. Mary letter to Board, Aug. 18, 1896.
13. Hoy letter to Board, May 19, Oct. 13, 1897; Dec. 5, 1898; *The*

Messenger, Sept. 30, 1897.
14. Hoy letter to Board, Sept. 28, 1896.
15. *Ibid.*, Dec. 11, 1896.
16. *The Messenger*, Nov. 4, 1897.
17. Hoy letter to Board, Feb. 22, 1897.
18. *Ibid.*, Jan. 15, Feb. 22, Mar. 3, 1897.
19. *Ibid.*, Mar. 3, 1897.
20. *Ibid.*, Sept. 8, 1897.
21. *Ibid.*, Nov. 6 and Dec. 11, 1897.
22. *Ibid.*, Mar. 8, Apr. 13, 15, 23, 29, 1897.
23. Hoy Annual Report 1897; Hoy letter to Board, May 27, 1898.
24. Hoy letter to Board. Aug. 10, 1898.
25. *Ibid.*, Nov. 23 and Dec. 11, 1898.
26. *Ibid.*, Aug. 10, 1898.
27. *Ibid.*, Nov. 21, 1898.
28. *Ibid.*, Feb. 9, 1898.
29. Mission Proceedings, Mar. 12, 1899; Hoy letter to Board, Apr. 18, 1897.
30. Hoy letter to Board. Nov. 6, 1897.
32. Mission Proceedings, Mar. 11 and Sept. 1899.
33. *Ibid*, Dec. 8, 1899.
34. Hoy. W.E., *History of the China Mission*, p. 49-50.

Chapter X - ANOTHER NEW BEGINNING

"I feel as if my youth were given back to me."
Hanyang, China-Jan. 12, 1900

After fifteen years of hardships, less rugged pioneers in their middle years with five young children would surely have settled for more comfortable Christian service back in Pennsylvania, but not William and Mary Hoy. Their missionary commitment had been, and still was, for life. In fact, it was the more severe rigors and appalling needs of China which beckoned them. The story of their China years, which covers the first quarter of the Twentieth Century, can only be told briefly here, for there is enough material in the archives for another volume. But that new beginning must be included here. Without it the story would be woefully incomplete.

This new beginning was from almost nothing. Unlike the first beginning, there was no invitation from Chinese Christians eager for help and no churches in Hunan to receive or assist them. Far more adverse were the conditions of housing and disease, the depressing poverty and filth, not to mention the hostility which could mean death. There were, however, a few missionaries of other denominations nearby who helped them get started. They also had the unreserved support of their own Mission Board, which they hadn't had the first time. The Hoys had become well known in the 'Home Church,' and therefore their new work in China enjoyed advantages that their pioneer activities in Japan had lacked. The Reformed Church had acted wisely in choosing veterans for this most demanding work.

Hoy proceeded alone immediately to Hankow in Hupeh Province where he arrived on November 15, 1899. In his first letter to the Board he was apologetic for having had to stay five days at the Grand Hotel at $7.00 per day. In Sendai the Methodist pastor had given him a letter of introduction to the Honorable A. Segawa, Consul for Japan in Hankow. The Consul, who was a Christian, received him as "a brother in Christ" and gave him a servant for two days to help in the search of a house. Hankow had had a great fire the year before, and nothing was available there, but across the Yangtse in Hanyang Hoy was able to rent a small house owned by the Wesleyan Mission. For four days, until the house was cleaned, he lived with the Cornabys, missionaries of that mission, who helped him much during the next few months. "The small house is half foreign and half native. Here I am living with one servant to do all the work of the house and kitchen. There are neither carpets on the floor nor pictures on the wall. I have only the most necessary pieces of furniture. In fact, I could almost imagine myself a monk practicing the simplest ways of life. When the proposed Mission is established I shall hope for a few more of the legitimate comforts of life." He began studying Chinese immediately with a teacher who was Christian.[1]

Hanyang served as the base from which Hoy went "prospecting" into nearby hostile Hunan. While studying the language he awaited the arrival of the Rev. Fred Cromer in March 1900 who was supported by Grace Church, Columbiana, Ohio. Hoy's letter, which was published in *The Messenger*, gives a vivid picture of the new situation in which he found himself.

Hankow, Hanyang and Wuchang form practically and commercially one great city. (Today collectively they are called Wuhan). It is said to be one of the great views of the world, to look down upon this busy emporium from the top of the hill near my little house. Hills, mountains, valleys, plains, the mighty Yangste, lakes, villages and the three large cities make up one of the most striking scenes on this beautiful globe. Every inch of ground seems to have its ancient history, and the spectator loses himself in the misty past.

For more than ten miles in various directions the surface of the countryside is covered with graveyards. There are millions sleeping in this great city of the dead. The graves look like beehives. Paved walks lead in all directions. Here I take my daily afternoon walks. Here I hear almost daily the jeering shout, "Foreign devil ? Kill the foreign devil !" I walk calmly and slowly on and leave the mocking crowd of the living behind me. The dead revile me not, neither do they laugh me to scorn. But their coffins in many places seem to ask for better burial. Many a coffin comes to view, as the ground crumbles away from the grave. The coffin soon rots if not recovered, and the bones lay bare. Ah, the old enemy Death has proof enough here of his victory over human flesh. We speak of the dead past and say that China is dead. Even among the living you can never be sure of being alone with the living. The dead may be present. For instance, you go to the living to rent a house. You are about to sign an agreement, when your companion discovers a sealed coffin in a small dark back room. The master tells you it cannot be removed, must not be removed, before the lucky time and place of burial can be determined by the priests. Not only in the house but also in the streets and in the graveyards one sees these coffins with the dead in them awaiting the priest's decision.

You are aware that the Chinese written language consists of

many tens of thousands of characters which are exceedingly difficult. Some of these are single characters and others are composed of several characters. The Chinese word for house, family, home, is made up by placing the character for roof over the one for pig. The pig is an animal with domestic rights. My neighbor's house consists of one large room. This is kitchen, dining room, parlor, bed room, and pig pen. In one corner of the room the mother pig and her little ones enjoy their comfortable bed of straw. In the home, on the streets, and in the shops, the pig roams, loafs, and grunts, with perfect liberty. I asked someone why the character for pig was used in spelling house. The answer came quickly. "The pig pays the rent."

Those of you who know somewhat of my suffering from most acute asthma in Japan will rejoice with me in the robust health I now enjoy. I usually express it this way, 'I eat like a healthy farmer, study like a true German, and sleep like an innocent child.' I do not even have troubled dreams, and I feel as if my youth were given back to me.[2]

Hoy also took a Chinese name which was necessary because the only way to write foreign names in Chinese is to assign characters in accordance with the pronunciation. So William E. Hoy became Hai Wei Li, the respective characters being those for sea, unite as cause and effect, and doctrine. Hoy was most pleased with the meanings conveyed by the three characters, doctrine united as cause to effect in the depth of the fullness of God like the sea.

Hoy strongly objected to the Board when he discovered that his salary in China was less. He attacked the idea of "living like the natives" and what he called "cheap missions." The Wesleyan Mission had lost fifteen missionaries in nine years as the result of such frugality. "Will any of the members of our church who are crying for cheap mission live with the pigs. I will not live on a lower physical basis than the common one I have all along adopted. Would to God I had wealth enough to be a missionary without being dependent upon people who seem to begrudge us every cent."[3]

Hoy's first visit to Hunan was in April 1900 when he went with Cromer to Yochow where Tung Ting Lake flows into the Yangtse. Two members of the London Mission had taken up residence there and a Chinese pastor helped them search for a place to purchase. They had decided it was "not wise to rent and be subject to any sudden change of mind on the part of a Chinese landlord who under the threat of parties hostile to us might suddenly turn us out at an unseemly hour."[4] But they postponed buying property because the prices were unreasonable. Yet they determined that Yochow would be a good base for future missionary operations in Hunan. Of one experience Hoy wrote,

> The first Sunday of our trip we stopped at a place called Peh-lu-si. We walked through an edge of the town, and passed on to the top of a hill nearby. A crowd of men, women, and children gathered around us. They were friendly enough at first; but as soon as we showed our backs to return to the boat they began to revile us. Presently mud and stones were thrown at us. I was struck on the right leg and on both shoulders. The nearer we got to the boat, the larger and noisier grew the rabble. Occasionally a voice would be lifted up, shouting, "Kill the foreign devils." After we reached our

boat, they continued to annoy us for a short time. Finally an official came upon the scene and scattered the crowd.[5]

Eager for his family to join him without delay, Hoy went to Kuling, the missionary vacation community in the mountains of neighboring Kiangsi Province, to buy a modest place to house his wife and children until proper arrangements could be made in Yochow, and because his little hovel in Hanyang was obviously not suitable. Then he and Cromer with their Chinese teacher went to Japan for the summer. Upon arrival in Nagasaki they learned about the Boxer Uprising in China which made it impossible for them to return that fall as planned. The summer was spent with the family at Takayama at the sea studying Chinese. In the fall the Hoys and Cromer moved to Kamakura where they continued their studies. Finally in February 1901 they were able to go to China. Mary and the children settled down in Kuling, while Hoy and Cromer went on to Yochow and with help from the two members of the London Missionary Society living there, they rented a humble dwelling. Years later Hoy recollected,

> Were we to describe minutely everything connected with that house and with our efforts to get it clean, it would be necessary to give you an ugly picture of filth, and, of course, the odors could not be put on paper. We lived right among the Chinese and soon learned what a Christless community means. It was a poor home, and yet in that house we made the real beginning of our work in the second land of my adoption, and fond recollections somehow cast a spell over the place, which life and work in more suitable environment cannot

break.   The place marks a starting point, and therein lies its value for me.⁶

Four times in three months they were molested by robbers. City officials sent twenty soldiers to guard the house. One night a robber left his sword behind when their servant awoke and chased him away, and after that Hoy slept with the sword at his side.⁷

Almost immediately after his arrival in China, Cromer began having trouble with his eyes which was greatly aggravated by his intense study of Chinese characters. Gradually it became apparent that he should not continue, and in November 1901 he finally resigned. Hoy had been highly appreciative of his young colleague, and his withdrawal was a disappointment. Hoy was now alone again, so he went to Kuling to get his family and they arrived back in Yochow two days before Christmas. After more than two years of sojourning the Hoy family had a home again together. The five children ranged from ages four to eleven, with William, 44, and Mary, 38, embarking upon a pioneer venture, in a new language and difficult situation.

The first Protestant missionary known to have entered Hunan was Reverend Josiah Cox of the Wesleyan Missionary Society in 1863. Eight years later Dr. Griffith John of the London Missionary Society made an extensive trip through the province, and then in 1875, Mr. C. H. Judd of the China Inland Mission rented property in Yochow but was soon driven out. It was not until 1897 that the first regular mission station was established in the province at Yochow by the London Missionary Society, with the first resident missionaries being the Rev. A.L. Greig and Dr. E.A. Peake, a physician. Within a few months of the Hoy's arrival, these two missionaries moved up the river to Hengchow and Hoy was able to buy their property. He also inherited one Christian, the first convert in Hunan who had been baptized the year before, and also several seekers. Thus April 1, 1902, the day the property was purchased, represented the official beginning of the China Mission of the Reformed Church in the U.S.[8]

One of Hoy's earliest activities was selling Christian literature, an activity which could be done with the minimum of language, yet one which provided excellent language training as well as contact with the people. In *The Messenger* he reported having thousands of Bibles and a variety of tracts on hand which he would take into the streets in a large bag strapped to his back. Of the difficulties he encountered he wrote,

> If you do not strengthen yourself with prayer, you will ever feel the impulse to turn your back on the filthy, ignorant, opium besotted, and scornful and agitated crowd. You will need the presence of the Holy Spirit to enable you to keep in mind the worth of a single soul. Rest assured that you will not go among these crowds "for the fun of it." "Pray without ceasing" and you will be borne along on a mighty current of persevering love.

His Chinese teacher was a proud Confucian scholar whose knowledge was limited to the Classics. He had only contempt for the ignorant masses, refused to acknowledge Hoy in public, and Hoy's servant looked down upon him for "becoming a merchant." But all of this only strengthened Hoy's Christian convictions. "The external cover of idolatry and superstitution cannot hide from the true child of God the idea and ideals of the divine in the brother Chinese, and one soon loves this new brother, not so much for what he now is, as for that which he may become in Christ."[9]

As in Sendai, the Hoys soon began teaching in their home. At first William had only four boys and Mary two girls, one of whom was the daughter of a prostitute. Unlike Japan it was hard to get students, especially girls, because according to a Chinese proverb which Hoy quoted, "Eighteen beautiful girls are not equal to one boy with a limp." Some parents said they would send their daughters but didn't. Finally Mary went out to gather any girls who would come, even without cost, which reminded her of Jesus' parable about the invited guests who didn't come. In September 1902 the Yochow Girls' School was started with five students and the Seek New Learning School with nine boys. William and Mary were repeating in Yochow what they had done in Sendai sixteen years previously under far less adverse circumstances.[10]

Tragedy struck the family on its way back from vacation in Kuling that summer of 1902. Seven-year-old David came down with cholera in Hankow, and though he received excellent and loving Christian care in the foreign hospital there he died within a week on September 18th, his fever intensified by the humid heat.[11] A dozen years later his father wrote,

> During that year your missionaries received the loving discipline

of the removal of little David. At that Hankow grave we obtained a new vision of Him who always doeth all things well. What was then and there learned has been used for the comfort of sorrowing Chinese. God is love even when we bury our dead. We see Him then face to face.[12]

The lad had wanted to be a doctor. That had often been his play, just like his father as a boy with preaching. Therefore quite fittingly, in 1907 the David Schneder Hoy Memorial Hospital was opened in Yochow with gifts from the Hoys' many friends in America.

In December 1902 five new missionaries arrived to augment the work. They were Miss Emma Ziemer for the girls' school, Rev. and Mrs. William Reimert for the boys' school, and Albert and Lillian Beam who were both physicians. The Beams arrived just in time to take care of Gertrude, ten, and Mabel, nine, who had typhoid. From the very beginning the need for medical work had been imperative. Dr. Peake, the predecessor of the Hoys, had operated a dispensary on the mission compound, and the sick continued to come there for help. He had also left some medicines and other supplies which William and Mary administered as best they could. But the need for a missionary doctor and better medical facilities was imperative. With the arrival of the Beams medical service became an important part of the Christian outreach of the China Mission of the German Reformed Church.[13]

The educational activities also grew. With Miss Ziemer as its first principal the girls' school gradually began to attract more students, even daughters from some leading families, especially after a building was erected in 1911. In 1907 the more rapidly growing boys' school was moved to a beautiful site outside the town on Tung Ting Lake, where Hoy planned and supervised the construction of the buildings. To the primary school was added a preparatory course of three years and an academy of four years. The name was changed to The Lakeside School and later to Huping Christian College. Instead of developing a seminary, which had been Hoy's priority in Japan, theological education was conducted in cooperation with the English Wesleyan Methodist Missionary Society, the American Presbyterian Mission, and the United Evangelical Mission Society through the formation of the Hunan Theological Seminary in Changsha, the capital of the province. Tragedy struck both Yochow schools in the second decade of their development. In 1913 Miss Ziemer drowned in a boat accident enroute with her students to attend a Christmas service at the boys' school. In her honor the school became known as the Ziemer Memorial Girls' School. Then on June 13, 1920, Rev. Reimert was martyred at the height of his career trying to protect the students from bandits at the East Gate of Huping College.[14]

Evangelistic work was central to the work. The first baptismal service was held for two men, two women and one child on the last Sunday of 1902. The first congregation was organized in Yochow with twelve members on February 15, 1903, in the presence of Rev. Arthur V. Casselman, the Field Secretary of the Mission Board. This marked the first visit of a board official to the Japan and China Missions. In 1904 a church building was erected, the pews a gift from Hoy's home church in Mifflinburg and the pulpit plus altar furniture, all handcrafted in Pennsylvania, were from Miss Ziemer's home church in Reading. Hoy often worked along with the coolies even in the summer heat because there was "no skilled labor and the missionary has to help the workmen sometime."[15] In *The Messenger* he commented, "All over the world there are those who spend their days in toil and heat. Let us not forget them. Substantial civilization is built up largely by labor that gets little praise and I fear, less sympathy. In the most illiterate workmen let us look for the image of God."[16] As in Sendai he lacked sufficient funds and did not hesitate to express his anger to the Board for the additional and unnecessary burden this imposed on him.[17] But he was much encouraged with what was happening. In his 1903 Annual Report he wrote,

> Six years ago Dr. John was stoned out of this city. Today we go unmolested wherever we please, and many of the citizens greet us pleasantly. Seldom do we hear a disrespectful word. We employ 100 men daily. Yochow officials have been uniformly kind and courteous to us. They are ever ready to do us favors, and pay us frequent calls. They seem grateful to us for the position which we have taken, never to interfere with their work and duties.

This latter comment referred in contrast to the stance taken by certain other missionaries, especially Catholics, who expected special treatment, and, if necessary, protection from their own governments. A year later, however, Hoy experienced some difficulty with an official in Chiangshi who dealt with him dishonestly, "in the rudest manner possible, heaping insult upon insult, purposely omitting common courtesies." Hoy appealed to the officials in Yochow, who promptly corrected the situation and removed the subordinate involved.[18] In the Yochow Field, as that area of the China Mission came to be known, there were twelve out-stations within twenty years in the surrounding countryside. Trips lasting several weeks, subject to the danger of capture by bandits for ranson, were made by the missionaries and Chinese evangelists. In 1923 there were seventeen Sunday schools and the Yochow Church had 410 members.[19]

A second center was opened in 1904 in western Hunan at Shenchow in the rugged country 300 miles west of Yochow. Two years previously two young missionaries of the China Inland Mission had been killed in a riot at that outpost. The British government had demanded an indemnity of $50,000 with the intention of using a large portion of it for the benefit of the people of Shenchow. The China Inland Mission had withdrawn from that area, and a Rev. William Kelley had moved in to work as an independent. The British offered him $30,000 for use in his work provided he became related to an established mission, whereupon he joined the Reformed Church Mission. The money was sufficient for the erection of two hospitals, one for men and another for women, since at that time the two sexes could not be mixed. Together they were known as Abounding Grace Hospital. Two schools were also started, the Eastview School for Boys and the Shenchow Girls' School. The town, which later was called Yuanling, also became the center of extensive evangelistic activity throughout that region. In September 1926 the Rev. Karl Beck and Miss Minerva Weil were captured by bandits and held in the mountains until the ransom of $3,000 was paid. In this Shenchow Field Hoy himself was not directly involved, although as senior missionary with two decades more experience than any of his colleagues, he was the dean of all the ventures. With the years he became for the China Mission of the German Reformed Church, even in a more singular way, what Schneder became for the Japan Mission, where there were two other veterans, Moore and Noss. All were eventually honored with honorary doctorates, Schneder in 1899 and Hoy in 1903 by Franklin and Marshall College and later Moore and Noss.[20]

A few footnotes on the desperate human scene give more substance to the tasks that beckoned, especially in the early years. No sooner had Hoy settled in Yochow than an illiterate old woman came to him for help, and he taught this eager student her first Chinese characters.[21] One day while selling books in the street he was confronted by a bully who grabbed the books from him and roughed him up a bit. But Hoy called the fellow's bluff and with humor diffused the potentially threatening crowd.[22] A man named Ma, a pathetic opium addict, came for help. After a week of the trauma of complete withdrawal as a patient on Hoy's veranda, the man was cured and eventually became one of the mission's most effective evangelists.[23] One morning Mrs. Hoy picked up a little boy whose head was a mass of scabs and his body covered with ulcers. She cleaned him up and put him in the boys' school. Eventually he became one of the leading educators and scientists of China. Then there was the little girl who was bought for two and a half dollars, and later became a teacher in a Christian school.[24]

As in Japan a chief concern was with the low estate of women, of which the custom of footbinding was the most glaring symbol. Although the mission schools did not require the girls to unbind their feet, all the students did eventually, as did those women who became Christian and many others who came under Christian influence. For Hoy the oppression of women was deeply rooted in wrong religion, yet he found much evidence for the resilience of his Chinese sisters.

> Let no one estimate the influence of woman in China too lowly. Has she not charge of the children, both sons and daughters, during the most impressionable age? Confucius may have relegated woman to an inferior position, but she has kept the grand old role of mother, which neither the slight passed upon her by Confucianism, nor the contempt involved in the Buddhist idea that she must be born again as a man in order to reach the state of Nirvana, can successfully deny her. The eternal power and influence of wife and mother are hers always and everywhere. There are homes where the maternal graces in all their pristine glory are not lost on account of the false position allotted to woman by the religions of the land. Woman in the faithful and humble performance of her natural functions is not so far from God as Confucius himself was. Both in Japan and China the eternal feminine has persisted through all the sins committed against woman by the sages, who led the better instincts of the masculine captive with the specious doctrine of the superiority of man over woman. Lost in speculation, the intellectual leaders of old China have left it to a deeper and more practical generation to develop the richest resources of the nation - her womanhood.[25]

The Protestant missionary movement had from its inception been unqualifiedly devoted to the importance of the family and to the vital role of the missionary wife, both inside and outside the home, while at the same time fully supporting the unique contributions of single women. From his perspective of nearly three decades, Hoy wrote,

> No Christian woman can witness unmoved the low position in which the religions of China have defined her sister's life and rights. Does a missionary's wife engage in woman's work ? You know the beautiful story of that American mother who rocked the cradle with one hand, and with the other took the pen and helped mightily to shake the old system of slavery to pieces. Likewise may you see on the mission field in all lands the double-handed love of the missionary's wife at home for her husband and children, and among the people for girls and women. Even where circumstances make it impossible for her to undertake the more consecutive form of evangelistic work, her occasional ministrations and constant presence by the side of her husband will always be a witnessing of Christ. The annals of missions are neither complete nor just without a true valuation of the missionary wife and mother. In this domestic strength on the field, Protestantism has a tremendous advantage over the system that demands the celibacy of the clergy.[26]

Little is known about the early education of the Hoy children, though undoubtedly it was in the able hands of Mary who was a trained and experienced teacher. Education by the mother was the traditional missionary pattern especially in the hinterland. Needless to say it was a monumental and time-consuming task, but the time inevitably came when the children had to go away to school. In 1904

Mary took the four children to America, and William went on furlough the following year stopping in Japan enroute. In welcoming him to the 'Home Church,' *The Messenger* proclaimed, "Hoy is a fanatic, a zealot, possessed of a great idea. Burning with great enthusiasm, he knew that what he was doing was wise and the will of God. What has taken us twenty-five years to do in Japan has been done in five years in Yochow."[27] Willie went to Mercersburg Academy and then to Franklin and Marshall College, eventually receiving his doctorate in biology from Princeton University. After his early teens he seldom was with his father. Gertrude and Mabel went to high school in Lancaster, while Charles went to high school in Princeton when his brother was in graduate school there. The education of the children required Mary to be in America for several years, leaving William alone in his work in Yochow.

Gertrude, after graduating from Hood College for Women in Frederick, Maryland, one of the educational institutions of the Reformed Church, became the first child of a missionary of that church to become a missionary. In 1913 at the age of 21 she became a teacher at the Yochow Girls' School which her mother had started, and within a few years was its principal. Mabel graduated from Oberlin College, a co-educational school of the Congregational Church in Ohio, and in 1914 became a teacher in a Presbyterian girls' school in Changsha, a few hours south of Yochow by train. There she met Nicolai Kiaer, a Norweigan Y.M.C.A. missionary whom she married in 1916. Trained as a kindergarten teacher, she taught her two daughters, Ruth, born in 1916 and Edle born in 1920.

A letter dated September 14, 1922 from William at Huping Christian College to his son, William, then teaching at Presbyterian College, Clinton, South Carolina, is worth quoting because it provides a more intimate glimpse of Hoy, along with an appraisal of the situation in which he was working at the time. Young William had just bought a new Ford and with his brother, Charles, had made a trip to Pennsylvania. This led the father to quip, "There are no automobiles in Yochow yet, but there 'auto' be!" The Huping School was full and new dormitories needed, but there was no money. A new missionary would soon arrive to replace Reverend Reimert, who had been martyred just two years previously. He was Hesser Ruhl, whose parents Hoy had grown up with in Mifflinburg. Huping had just had another bout with bandits who were trying to capture Hoy because they believed he would bring a large ransom, but "Mr. Lequear's three shots on the first night that the bandits made their appearance scared then off because they knew there were four foreigners here and about sixty teachers and students." Yet the bandits kept prowling the neighborhood. "I do not know how much of a fight I would show, but I believe that Mr. Lequear and Mr. Beck would sell their lives very dearly, being well armed." This led Hoy to comment,

> It is awful to speak about, but I think that the same condition that prevails in the class-room obtains outside in the affairs of politics and crime. You will have no trouble in a class-room filled with Chinese boys if you are not afraid to use Roosevelt's Big Stick. Your dad has the reputation of being a good whip. I keep a tough

creeper vine which is very flexible, and when I strike a good blow on the table with it, it is like the report of a gun. When I bring it down on the table in the presence of a stubborn boy who has been sent to me for correction, he soon says, "I'll be good." On one occasion I used an edged ruler and while I was spanking the back of the boy's hand the edge covered with brass cut his hand and drew blood. Then I had to play the part of the Good Samaritan. I washed the wound, cleaned off the blood ; I did not pour oil on it but bound up the hand. By the time we had finished we were good friends, and that boy has not made me any trouble since. I think my attending to his slight injury touched him and influenced him more than the thrashing did.

This experience led him to observe about the situation in general,

Unity of purpose seems impossible, and the unification of the provinces is a problem that I cannot solve. There are leaders who have honest purposes but there are not enough of them. The average Chinese is a personification of selfishness. The people at large are considered the prey of those who are war lords and they are looted, robbed, and murdered, if necessary, by these traitors whose one thought is money. When they have gotten the money, they say, "Come let us built a palace, let us establish a harem," and there is where the trouble lies. But I believe that a better day is coming. I have profound faith in the ability and the vision of the rising generation of Chinese men. It is the old conservatives, wallowing in the mire of their own pollution, that keep back the unification of the country. Even Sun Yat Sen, the supposed great patriot of China, has fallen more or less a victim to the actions of the war lords. However, the Christian forces are being consolidated, are working more and more in unity of purpose, and there is a great progress made in medical, educational, and evangelistic work. All of these forms of service for the establishment of the Kingdon of God you will find locally, and many of the troubles which the war lords are bringing to bear upon the people impel them to seek peace and rest in God, and under the comforts of the Christian religion they suffer patiently the evils that are thrust upon then.

A year later tragedy struck the family again. Charles, the youngest child, had become a natural scientist of the prestigious Smithsonian Institute in Washington D.C. In 1919 he had been sent on an expedition to Australia to search for endangered species, his shipments eventually totalling 571 mammals and 534 birds. Then in 1922 he was sent to China where he worked first in the Yochow area and next in Kiangsi province which was in such turmoil that a military escort was needed. On one trip in a remote area he suffered an accidentally self-inflicted gun wound in his foot, and not long thereafter a ruptured appendix which took his life on Setember 6, 1923, just three weeks before his twenty-sixth birthday. Some of his specimens are still on exhibit in the Smithsonian Museum.[28]

In 1924 William and Mary took their fourth furlough which proved to be their last. Enroute to America they spent the month of July in Japan, staying in Sendai with the Gerhards, Blanche Gerhard being Mary's youngest sister. At Shiroishi a union service was held, with people baptized by Hoy coming from such near-by towns as Ogawara, Murata, Iwanuma, Kakuda, and Watari. A similar visit was made to the Fukushima Church, and then with Noss to Wakamatsu.

They also visited Yamagata, Sakata, Akita, Aomori and Ishinomaki. Since Hoy had not used Japanese for a quarter of a century he preached through interpreters. In Sendai he gave lectures at both of the schools he had helped found, and Mary spoke to women's groups in many places. Their subject was, of course, their Christian work in China. They also were warmly entertained at two festive parties in Sendai, one given by Tohoku Gakuin and the other by the churches in the area.[29]

As they approached their senior years the fruit of their labors as pioneers in the hinterlands of the two great countries of East Asia was both abundant and much appreciated. In 1925 before returning to China, Heidelberg College, the Reformed Church institution in Tiffin, Ohio, conferred upon Hoy the honorary degree of Doctor of Laws.[30]

Footnotes

1. Hoy letter to Board, Nov. 26, 1899; Hoy, *History of China Mission*, p. 51.
2. Hoy letter to Board, Jan. 12, 1900.
3. *Ibid.*, Dec. 2, 1899.
4. Hoy, *History*, p. 55.
5. Hoy letter to Board, Jan. 1900.
6. Hoy, *History*, p. 58.
7. Bartholomew, Tribute to Hoy.
8. Hoy, *History*, p. 61f and 90f.
9. *The Messenger*, Mar. 6, 1902.
10. *Ibid.*, Jan. 29, 1903; Hoy, *History*, p. 74f. Casselman, *Hunan*, p. 127f.
11. *Forward*, Foreign Mission Day Service, Feb. 8, 1903, p. 10.

12. Hoy, *History*, p. 73 ; Casselman, *Hunan*, p. 205.
13. Casselman, *Hunan*, 205f.
14. *Ibid.*, 132f.
15. Hoy Annual Report 1903.
16. *The Messenger*, Aug. 4, 1904.
17. *Ibid.*
18. *Ibid.*, Dec. 8, 1904.
19. Hoy, *History*, p. 93f. and Casselman, *Hunan*, p. 88f.
20. Hoy, *History*, p. 79f. and Casselman, *Hunan*, p. 99f. and 148f.
21. Hoy, *History*, p. 69.
22. *Ibid.*, p. 65.
23. *Ibid*, p. 116f.
24. Casselman, *Hunan*, p. 70.
25. Hoy, *History*, p. 65–66.
26. *Ibid.*, p. 67–68.
27. *The Messenger*, May 18, 1905.
28. Hoy Family Records.
29. Tsuchida, *Hoy Japan Visit*, T.G.U. Archives.
30. *The Messenger*, Mar. 17, 1927.

Chapter XI - THE LAST BEGINNING

"One year and a half ago we returned to a rapidly changing China. We may be too old to readjust ourselves to our new environment, but this inability must not embitter us. Should we be driven out tomorrow, our Labor in the Lord has not been in vain." Yochow, China. Nov. 1926.

A year after the Hoys returned from furlough China was engulfed in the turmoil of civil war. For years the country had been torn by the rivalry of the warlords, while the government in Peking proved unable either to maintain domestic order or to resist the intrusion of the Western powers. In Kwangtung in the south the Kuomingtang consolidated its power in coalition with the emerging Communists in order to bring about a revolution and unify the country. In the summer of 1926 the Nationalist armies under Chiang Kai-shek began a triumphant march northward through Hunan to Hankow, much aided by trained agitators who directed popular sentiment against the unequal treaties, attacking foreign merchants and Christian institutions as agents of imperialism. These agitators also organized laborers and peasants against employers and landlords, and in places like Hunan a reign of terror followed, in which many of the propertied class were dispossessed and even executed. Since the Communist stronghold was in Hunan, the situation there became chaotic, especially in Yochow because of its geographical position on the Yangtse and on the main railroad between Canton and Peking. By December the

Communists were largely gaining control. One of Hoy's junior colleages, Dr. Paul V. Taylor, years later described the scene graphically.

Central China was in the throes of another revolution. This time the issue was Communism, with a capital C. There was a regular patrol around the campus wall. No one was permitted to leave or enter.

By Christmas time the whole countryside was seething with hatred. The venerable president of the college, Dr. W.E. Hoy, a man who had devoted his life to unselfish mission work and built this school from its foundation, and who was to retire at that the end of the current school year, came running up the walk calling to me. We were there at lunch. He was bareheaded and very much excited. 'Help! Come! I need help!' he called. 'These boys for whom I have done everything and to whom I have devoted my life, have turned against me.' I went with him to his office, and it was even as he had said. Men and boys who had been most friendly, with whom we had played basket-ball, tennis and soccer, who had sat in our classes, eager to learn all they could, who had attended a party in my home two nights previously, who had sat as inquirers in my class in religious training - these men now hated us as if we had done them the most severe injustice.

A Student Union had been formed. This organization took over the Middle School and the College. They hired and fired teachers. They told the teachers how to teach and when. We, as foreigners, as representatives of Imperialism, were out. The Communist army was daily coming closer.[1]

To the Board Secretary Hoy wrote,

Whatever may come to us, please remember that Mrs. Hoy and I do not regret our having served so long in this land. Service has been joy. One year and a half ago we returned to a changed and rapidly changing China. We may be too old to readjust ourselves to the new environment, but surely this inability must not embitter us. Both God and man have been gracious to us all our years in this land of the Far East. In all our efforts we have tried to hold up Christ and Him crucified, and we still believe in Him who was sent into the world to save those who receive him. Should we be driven out tomorrow, our labor in the Lord has not been in vain. In these discouraging days there are many in China who by letter and by personal calls testify to what the Christ preached or taught means. For all this we take heart and rejoice for the service the Lord has owned. Let not the Board and Church become discouraged. God's right arm of salvation has not been shortened. The Church still lives."[2]

On January 8th the missionary women and children, along with some men, were evacuated on a small British steamer. Within a few days it became imperative for those who remained to leave with haste. In the archives is a poignant photo of the elderly Hoy being led up a narrow gang plank to a junk by a coolie wading in the water. For the first two days the trip down the Yangtse was perilous with snipers as far as Hankow where an armed vessel took them safely to Shanghai. Over 3,000 missionaries fled China that year. Throughout the province of Hunan all Christian schools and hospitals were shut down and many chapels desecrated. At first some Christian teachers and students were quite sympathetic toward the communists but many soon became disillusioned and some were severely persecuted. On the otherhand, the same was often true where the Kuomingtang was in control. Dr. Paul E. Keller, a veteran colleague of Hoy's since 1905, described the essence of the crisis clearly.

> This is a day of uncertainty. But this people is fighting for a better day and our sympathies must be with them. If in the meanwhile they do foolish things, so did the western nations. Of course, the Red influence is being used to upset everything. The Church's indifference to the common people's rights and interests has raised a monster in Russia that is troubling the churches of all lands. The sufferings and injustices of Eastern people have made them see Red. Other nations have had similar experiences and they have acted on their feelings and done worse than the Chinese are doing now. However, for the present there is no possibility of doing anything in Hunan. It is rather difficult to reason with a herd of stampeding buffaloes. For the present one has to step out of the direct line of rush. In the end hatred must crush itself. We are praying for that day, not merely waiting for it.[3]

Hoy, broken in spirit and failing in body, sailed from Shanghai with Mary and Gertrude. When their ship stopped in Yokohama, their old friend, David Schneder, was there to meet them. But William was weak and confined to bed. On March 3, 1927, a few days from Portland, he died peacefully at age 68 with his wife and daughter at his side. One account holds that the ship doctor told Gertrude, "This man need not have died. There was no organic reason for his death. He died of a broken heart." But the official record listed the cause of his death as a stroke.[4] The Kiaer family who had also fled

China were on a ship nearby, and the four of them were able to transfer at sea to the other ship. The funeral was held in the Mifflinburg Church with burial in the cemetery there. On May 10th a memorial service was held in the chapel of the seminary in Lancaster. The eulogies, both spoken and written, came from three countries. But as Hoy often put it, he was a citizen of four countries, not only America, Japan, and China, but most importantly, the Kingdom of God. The sermon entitled, "A Voice Eloquent in Death," was by Dr. Allen R. Bartholomew, who had been part-time Secretary of the Board from 1887 to 1890 and then full-time from 1902. Quoting Hoy's critical letters for pleas for help in the early years, he added,

> I find comfort for myself in the thought that in spite of all the handicaps that were thrown around the years of Dr. Hoy in Japan, the results since prove that he was right in blazing the path of duty of our Church and the Board, and how faith wrought with his works was made perfect.[5]

One appraisal by a Mission Board member put his greatness quite candidly, "William Hoy had his faults, but they were all on the right side." Hoy left no estate except his accomplishments in Japan and China, along with the "awakening of the Home Church" to the world's needs and to a wider understanding of God's love and purpose.[6]

Mary Hoy returned to Yochow in June 1929 at the age of 66 soon after the doors began to open. Along with the other missionaries she was warmly welcomed. In her typical way of understatement she wrote the Board, "Our good friends have not changed, but conditions have and it is going to take some time to get adjusted." The losses and damages sustained in the two years were extensive. According to the official estimate of the China Mission, the loss in the Yochow Field was $32,352 and in the Shenchow Field, $79,825, which represented a huge sum of money for the small church at home. Many of the mission buildings had been badly abused. Horses had been kept in one of the finest rooms in the Ziemer Girls' School.[7] Reconciliation and reconstruction were the order of the day.

William Jr., professor of biology at the University of South Carolina, had hoped that his mother and sister would remain in America where Gertrude could have obtained a college position. But Gertrude's heart was in China too, and back she went to the Ziemer Girls' School. Nicolai Kiaer returned to Hunan in 1929, leaving Mabel in Norway because of the education of their two daughters. In 1934 tragedy struck the family again when Nicolai drowned in Tung Ting Lake at age 46. Ironically, he had been in in the 1912 Olympics, in diving, gymnastics, and ski jumping. Mabel spent the rest of her long life in Norway, much loved by the people of the fourth country in her life. She died in 1971 in Oslo where for years she was manager of the Missionary Home.[8] Her daughter, Ruth Tollefsen, who has three sons and four grandchildren, lives in Oslo. Her other daughter, Edle Waerum, lives in Namsos in the north.[8]

Mary's last trip to the United States was in 1933 with Gertrude on furlough. Again the family hoped she would remain, but again she returned, with Gertrude. This time a menace from outside was threatening, which led to war when a clash occurred on July 7, 1937 between Chinese and Japanese troops in the Peking area. The vastly superior Japanese army advanced rapidly at first into the interior. By early September Japanese planes were attacking Yochow, and Mary's health was rapidly declining. From Rev. Sterling Whitener in Yochow the Mission Board received the following word, "Mrs. Hoy has had a very bad time during the past two weeks, since her birthday on September 10th. When the air raid alarm sounded, Miss Hoy moved her mother to the basement under the Girls' School dormitory. The excitement of that move had made her much worse, so Dr. Li has strongly advised that she should not be moved again. He considers the danger from bombing less than the danger of moving." Then on December 5th a cable was received. "Mary Hoy died today." She was buried in Hankow with David and Charles. Again the eulogies were many and from three countries. By nature she was modest, but she had absolutely nothing at all about which to be modest. Without her there would not have been the William who is celebrated in one of the stained glass windows of the chapel at the Mercersburg Academy along with other towering Christians like St. Paul, Constantine, Livingstone and Grenfell. Those who knew Mary well described her as winsome and diligent with exceptional intellectual ability, and above all a great and encompassing heart. Many, from the lowest to the highest, called her 'Mother Hoy.'[9] The ironical circumstances of her death, when one country she loved was bombing another country she loved, made poignant the need for the Gospel which she had proclaimed from youth and by which she had lived until she died at age 74.

Gertrude's life deserves another book. Made of the same substance as her parents, she persevered through new trials and dangers which they had never known. Small of body she was large in spirit and tough in both. Faith and hope, much tested, remained undaunted. After her mother's death, refugees began pouring into Hunan ahead of the advancing Japanese army. Huping College, Ziemer Girls' School, and the David Schneder Hoy Memorial Hospital were filled to overflowing. As the attacks on Yochow increased the two schools were moved across Tung Ting Lake to Lo Gia Dzui. On July 20th Yochow was badly bombed and left almost deserted. With the city about to fall to the Japanese, the hospital was closed and as much of the equipment as possible moved by boat 300 miles up the river to Yuanling. Miss Mary Myers and Rev. Karl Beck stayed behind in Yoohow to work under the Japanese occupation. Some of the mission buildings had been destroyed, others were badly damaged, and a few were torn down to use the bricks. Mission houses were looted and a chapel was used to house prostitutes. With the advance of the Japanese army the country was being divided into two constantly changing parts, Occupied China and Free China. Yochow, where the Hoys had worked, was in the former part, and Yuanling, where the two schools soon fled, was in the latter part. Then on August 18, 1939 Yuanling was bombed and Gertrude moved her school another 100 miles into the rugged mountains to Yangsui, using simple huts and often even caves. Yuanling was often bombed but never taken, so it became the center of the China Mission of the Reformed Church until the war was over. On December 8, 1941, Miss Myers and Rev. Beck in

Yochow were placed in internment by the Japanese, and then repatriated from Hong Kong on the Asama Maru with many missionaries from the Japan Mission, the Ankeneys, the Robert Gerhards, the Schroers, and Mrs. Nicodemus. The ship sailed to Lorenzo Marques in Portuguese East Africa where it met a ship from America with Japanese internees. Gertrude and other missionaries remained in Free China.[10]

Soon after the Japanese surrender in August 1945 Gertrude and other missionaries returned from western Hunan to Yochow. The destruction of mission property was extensive, and the buildings that were left were full of filth. The lovely lakeside campus of Huping Christian College was described as 'a wilderness' with almost all the trees cut down. Meanwhile, in Sendai the two schools which Hoy had helped found had been reduced to ruins by American bombers on the night of July 9, 1945. Thus, through the folly of war, sixty years of work by the Reformed Church in East Asia had been severely ravaged. Both of the Hoys and the Schneders had been spared the final horror. The new tasks of reconstruction were undertaken by their able daughters, Gertrude in Yochow, and Margaret Schneder Ankeney in Sendai, and by a host of others including a new generation of post-war missionaries. Again, the people in the Home Church responded to the challenge.

For Gertrude, however, with one crisis past, another appeared. It was a kind of replay of 1927, but with a mounting communist victory over the Kuomingtang. Again Gertrude fled, just before 'the liberation.' In the fall of 1949 she came to Sendai to teach English at

Miyagi Gakuin which her father had founded. In 1958 she was called to the True Light School for Girls in Hong Kong. She retired in 1960 and spent a year with Mabel in Oslo. But in 1962 she went back to Hong Kong for another three years. When she finally retired in Lancaster she had served for forty-six years. After that she worked in the archives of the seminary library, while living in a small missionary apartment nearby. This writer, who had known her in Sendai, was her neighbor on his 1969-70 furlough. She was like a grandmother to his small children. On one occasion we invited Mrs. Ankeney and Katherine Zierdt, a retired nurse of the China Mission, to a dinner party. Much of the conversation was about Japan. At one point the two China veterans had a brief exchange in Chinese in obvious disagreement over something that had been said. But Gertrude never talked about what she and her Chinese colleagues had experienced under the Japanese. She died in the Annville Home on March 28, 1980, the last of the Hoy children, and was buried in Lancaster. Two generations of Hoys had spanned almost a century of Christian service in the two great countries of East Asia.

Dr. William Edwin Hoy. Jr. died in 1973. His daughter, Dr. Mary Camilla Hoy, is Professor of French and Spanish at Greensboro College in North Carolina, and his son, Dr. William Edwin Hoy, who is a physician in Ashland, Kentucky, has two sons and one daughter. In Mifflinburg are other Hoys, two of whom live on the family homestead.

The Hoy family is in possession of a sword which its oral tradition says was given to William by the Meiji Emperor. No record has been found of this, either in the mission archives or in the Japanese

Department of Foreign Affairs in Tokyo. But even if it was the gift of some lesser personage, it surely represents a most deserved token of a grateful people.

Thus ends a tale, which if it were fiction, would sound contrived. William and Mary would say it was the handiwork of God.

Footnotes

1. Casselman, *Hunan*, p. 257 f.
2. Bartholomew, A.R. *Memorial for Hoy*, p. 22.
3. Casselman, p. 257.
4. Hoy Family Records.
5. Bartholomew, *Memorial*, ö. 15.
6. Casselman, p. 41.
7. Ibid., p. 256-59.
8. Hoy Family Records.
9. *Ibid*.
10. Casselman, p. 260.

POSTSCRIPT

The story continues, the scene much changed. In this post-war era the two giants of East Asia have taken quite different paths which, in turn, have radically affected the work started by the Hoys in both countries.

Japan has risen from the ashes of its folly through its much heralded economic miracle to join the ranks of the so-called advanced nations. The prosperity wrought by capitalist expansion at home and abroad has transformed the country into one of the leading economic powers of the world. Poverty has been eliminated, and the standard of living is good for most people and high for some, with ninety percent identifying themselves as middle class. Consumer goods along with luxuries are in abundance, although prices are high. Influence from America as well as Western Europe has been massive, and much welcomed. A new kind of society is emerging which represents a strange mix of traditional and imported elements. Modernization has greatly promoted the foreign aspects which, however, are no longer considered alien, though the cherished heart of things remains distinctively Japanese. Democracy is still not deeply rooted, but the commitment of most people to more liberal values is growing steadily within a context which remains basically conservative. With the new affluence and freedoms have come many of the disruptions which have long plagued the West. Yet the social fiber remains strong, with the people confidently determined to advance carefully along the current course which has proved so successful.

The two schools in Sendai reflect these unprecedented developments. Both are self-supporting, self-governing, and much expanded with excellent modern facilities. Both have maintained their Christian identities, though somewhat diminished, with chapel services, required courses in Christianity and a variety of extra-curricular activities. The top administrators are Christian, as is at least one-tenth of the teaching staffs. Missionary colleagues are much desired, and for more than a decade much of their financial support has been provided by the schools. Tohoku Gakuin now includes a university, in addition to junior and senior high schools and even a kindergarten. With a total of about 14,000 students, one-tenth of whom are women, it is located on four campuses, the two older ones in the center of the city, and the other two in the suburbs. The university has departments in literature, economics, commerce, law and technology, as well as a small graduate division which offers a doctorate. Within the Department of Literature is a small Christian Studies Division with a faculty of thirteen Japanese and one missionary, who have the basic responsibility for the Christian program.

Miyagi Gakuin for Women with about 3,500 students is comprised of junior and senior high schools, a two-year junior college and a four year college, with departments in English literature, Japanese literature, home economics, and music, plus a Kindergarten Teacher Training Course with an attached day nursery school. In 1980 the school moved to a spacious campus with splendid facilities in the suburbs, surely one of the most beautiful educational institutions in the country. This spectacular development was made possible by selling the downtown site, long since crowded and inadequate. The result undoubtedly represents one of the most profitable investments in the history of missions, considering the fact that the original portion of that land was purchased for $1,400 in 1888. In short, the dramatic development of both schools during the past three decades has been a product of the rapid economic expansion of the country.

In similar fashion the radically different path taken by China has even more profoundly affected the work initiated by the Hoys in Yochow. Now that the country is opening, this writer was able recently to realize his ambition from childhood to visit that most ancient civilization of the world. With his wife and son he was able to travel quite freely into the hinterland with the masses on the jam packed transports, largely avoiding the foreign tourist routes. The accomplishments of liberation are many and impressive, since the exploitation of the masses by the wealthy few as well as by the foreign powers has ended. Though still poor by so-called First World standards, abject poverty has been abolished. No filth or fleas or flies, while the beggars and pathetic looking types a la Third World countries, not to mention any inner city of America, are conspicuous by their absence. The masses enjoy the basic necessities of life, including health care and education, which is free through the university for the few who pass the tests. Motor vehicles are few, and nothing is wasted, with engines turned off on any decline. Most work is done by personpower, consumer goods are at a premium, and night life is non-existent. Feudal structures have been discarded, and equality between the sexes largely achieved. The revolution involved every area of life to produce a highly egalitarian society. The people project an image of well-being and proud satisfaction with all the advances which have been so rapidly made. Most importantly, these achievements are the result, not of overseas exploitation but of domestic reform, though the price exacted was often oppressive and extreme, peaking in the ten-year reign of terror during the Cultural Revolution. But in recent years the new leaders have modified the course, granting increasing freedom and opening the country to foreign trade and influence. The standard of living is rising to include some of the formerly denounced frills. Communism in China is in transition along lines which are encouraging.

One of the purposes of this writer's trip was to visit Yochow, now called Yueyang, a rural town of 200,000 with the beginnings of industrialization. The old section between the railroad and the lake is congested but, except for dust, quite pleasant. On the narrow tree lined main street is the much expanded medical facility formerly known as the David Schneder Hoy Memorial Hospital. Actually it had only been a clinic. Above the door of the old building is a stone plaque from which the inscription has been erased. Nearby stands the first church which is still being used by the police, though it is scheduled to be returned for Christian purposes. Not far away is the former Ziemer Girls' School, now a middle school with 1,500 boys and girls, the old buildings badly neglected. Across the tracks new apartments and other buildings are under construction with bamboo scaffolds, at a pace which is relaxed. Foreigners are rare enough to be much stared at, a crowd soon assembling with the inevitable student eager to practice English. As everywhere there were always people who were friendly and helpful, by no means reluctant to associate with foreigners.

The highlight of the trip was the morning at the Huping (Lakeside) School about thirty minutes over dirt roads south of town. It is a lovely wooded site with cool breezes from the huge lake. Now it is a training school for about one hundred men and women cadres who stay for three months to two years. The original name of the school has been retained with the word, Christian, removed. The old buildings are intact, though in bad repair, but because they were well-built they are being slowly renovated. We had tea with Director Shi Cuo Pan, age fifty, in Hoy's former residence, now the administration building. For more than an hour we conversed through the guide we procured just for that day. I told about Hoy and the early work to uplift the people through education, medicine and social services. Director Shi spoke much about "people to people diplomacy." When we made a gesture to leave, he insisted that we stay for the lunch which was being prepared. So in the Spartan dining hall seated around a small table on narrow saw-horse benches eight of us enjoyed a Chinese feast complete with beer and rice wine and many toasts. From the windows and the vaulted ceiling, as well as the tower, it was obvious that we were in the former chapel, Christians and Communists breaking rice together in a house dedicated to the Glory of God. William and Mary Hoy would surely share our mixed feelings, glad for all the advances that have been achieved in the common struggle to improve life, but sad that the One behind it all still remains unknown. Yet around that table we were kindred spirits rejoicing in all that we could share. Later we wondered if the unexpected hospitality was an expression of gratitude for everything long since appropriated.

A week later we attended church in Hangzhou, a city a bit larger than Sendai. When we arrived at the Si Cheng Church, formerly Presbyterian, just before 8 a.m. the first service had already begun. We were led up front with people on the aisles reaching out to touch us, some with tears in their eyes. The sanctuary was filled with about 800 people, most of whom were older, as were the two pastors. The singing was robust and the sermon was animated and full of humor. When we parted one of the pastors said to me, "Pray for us." That day there were two more services. The city now has four functioning churches, all of which are prospering. Throughout the country 1,800 churches have been opened since 1979, with about one new opening a day. The number of Christians has more than tripled since liberation. The Nanjing Seminary is full with about 250 students. Most importantly, Christianity is no longer considered foreign. Its long association with western imperialism has been broken and denominationalism removed. The Protestants have formed the Three-Self Patriotic Movement Church to indicate that Christianity is self-supporting, self-governing, self-propagating and dedicated to the improvement of Chinese society. This represents a fundamental transformation with which the Hoys would also surely rejoice. In the process, however, the Christians suffered much. But the Faith not only survived, it was also strengthened. The Christ is very much alive in China and the few reapers of the mounting harvest are busy.

While William and Mary Hoy made no pretense in knowing how God would work out the divine purpose, either in Japan or China, they never for one moment doubted that God would, because throughout their lives they had experienced that redeeming power.

MAPS

PENNSYLVANIA

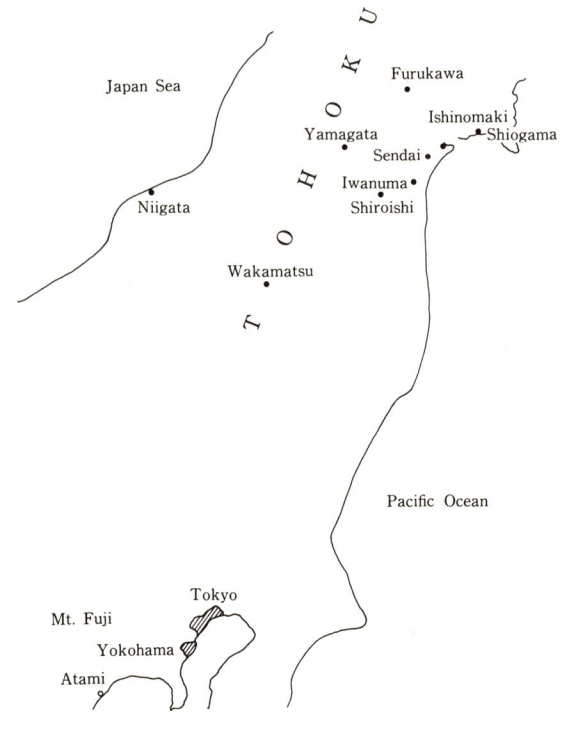

CHRONOLOGY

1858 - June 4 - William Hoy born in Mifflinburg, Pennsylvania.
1863 - Sept. 10 - Mary Ault born in Mechanicsburg, Pennsylvania.
1877 - Church of Christ in Japan (Union Church) founded by American Presbyterians Scottish Presbyterians, and Reformed Church in America.
1879 - Ambrose and Hattie Gring arrive as first missionaries to Japan of the German Reformed Church of the U.S. to work in Tokyo.
1880 - Oshikawa moves from Niigata to Sendai.
1881 - Sendai Church organized.
1883 - Jairus and Annie Moore arrive as second missionaries of German Reformed Church.
1885 - April - Hoy, Ault, Poorbaugh appointed missionaries to Japan.
June - Hoy graduates from Lancaster Seminary. Ault graduates. from Kutztown Teachers' College
December - Hoy arrives in Japan, meets Oshikawa. Japan Mission of Reformed Church organized.
1886 - Jan. - Hoy begins work in Sendai.
April - Japan Mission of Reformed Church joins Union Church.
June - Theological Training School of Sendai begins at Kimachi Kita Rokubancho.
July - Ault and Poorbaugh arrive in Sendai.
Sept - Girls' School begins at Higashi Yonbancho.
October - Toka Gakko begun by Congregational Board and Sendai officials.
1887 - Mar. - Board purchases Higashi Sanbancho lot for Girls' School. Theological Training School moves to house next to Girls' School.
Nov. - Sendai Church purchases Buddhist temple at Minami Machi Dori.
Dec. - Schneders arrive and Hoy-Ault wedding in Tokyo. Dai

	Ni Koto Chu Gakko started.
1888 - Aug. -	Hoy purchases at own expense part of lot of Sendai Church to erect Ault Memorial Hall.
-	Preparatory Department added to Theological Training School.
1889 - Jan. -	Completion of new Girls' School Building, two missionary residences, and Ault Memorial Hall.
May. -	Gring resigns.
1891 - Sept. -	Completion of new seminary building. Name changed to Tohoku Gakuin, officially rated as school of higher education.
1892 - Mar. -	Closing of Toka Gakko.
June -	Poorbaughs resign effective the following year. Opening of Shokei Jogakko by American Baptists.
1893 -	Beginning of work in Nagamachi. Shirayuri Girls' School begun by Catholics.
1895 - 1896 -	Hoy furlough.
1897 - Feb. -	Nagamachi Church dedicated, gift of Hoys. Sendai Siritsu Girls' High School founded. (first government school for girls.)
1898 - Spring -	Hoy's health trip to China. Oshikawa's leave of absence.
1899 - Oct. -	Hoy starts work in Hunan Oshikawa resigns.
1902 -	Schneder becomes president of Tohoku Gakuin.
1903 -	Hoy awarded Doctor of Divinity Degree in absentia by Franklin and Marshall College.
1925 -	Hoy awarded Doctor of Laws degree by Heidelberg College.
1927 - Feb. -	Hoys flee Hunan.
Mar. 3 -	William Hoy dies at sea.
1929 - Sept. -	Mary Hoy returns to China.
1937 - Nov. 5 -	Mary Hoy dies in Hankow.

BIBLIOGRAPHY

A History of the Evangelical and Reformed Church Christian Education Press, Philadelphia, 1961.

Bartholomew, A.R. *Won by Frayer*, the Life and Work of Rev. Masayoshi Oshikawa, Reformed Church Publications, Philadelphia, 1889.

Callender, S.N. *Historical Sketch of Work of Foreign Missions of Reformed Church in U.S.*, Phila. 1895.

Cary, Otis. *A History of Christianity in Japan* Revell Co., N.Y., 1909.

Casselman, Arthur V. *The End of the Beginning* Heidelberg Press, Philadelphia, 1936. *It Happened in Hunan*, Continental Press, Philadelphia, 1953.

DeForest, Charlotte B. *The Evolution of a Missionary*, Revell Co., N.Y. 1914.

DeForest, John H. *Sunrise in the Sunrise Kingdom*, Young People's Missionary Movement of U.S. and Canada, 1904.

Fifty Years of Foreign Missions of the Reformed Church in the U.S. 1877-1927, Board of Foreign Missions, Philadelphia-1904.

Hoy, William E., *Correspondence with Foreign Mission Board of the Reformed Church in the U.S. 1884-1901*, Archives of Lancaster Theological Seminary, Lancaster, Penn. and Tohoku Gakuin University, Sendai, Japan. *History of the China Mission of the Reformed Church in the U.S.*, Board of Foreign Missions, Philadelphia, 1914.

Mensendiek, C.W. *A Man for His Times*, The Life and Thought of David B. Schneder, Tohoku Gakui University, 1972.

Miller, Henry K., *History of the Japan Mission of the Reformed Church in the U.S. 1879-1904*, Board of Foreign Missions,

Philadelphia, 1904.

Moore, Jairus P. *Forty Years in Japan, 1883-1923*, Board of Foreign Missions, Philadelphia, 1925.

Noss, Christopher, *Tohoku, the Scotland of Japan*, Board of Foreign Missions, Philadelphia, 1914.

Official Proceedings of the Japan Mission of the Reformed Church in the U.S. 1885-1900, Archives of Lancaster Theological Seminary and Tohoku Gakuin University

Schroer, Cornelia R., *They Dared Live Their Faith*, Christian Women's Conference, 1979.

The Missionary Guardian of the Reformed Church

The Reformed Church Messenger

The Japan Evangelist

About the Author:

C. WILLIAM MENSENDIEK is Professor of Christian Studies at Tohoku Gakuin University and a missionary of the United Church of Christ. This church represents a merger in 1957 of the Congregational Christian Church and the Evangelical and Reformed Church. This latter church in turn represented a merger between the German Evangelical Church and the German Reformed Church in 1934. Dr. Mensendiek is the son of a pastor of the German Evangelical Church. He was born in Iowa, raised in Illinois, graduated from Elmhurst College in Elmhurst, Illinois in 1945 and from Eden Seminary in Webster Groves, Missouri in 1948, both of which were institutions of the Evangelical Church. On June 10, 1948 he was ordained into the ministry of the Evangelical and Reformed Church, and that September arrived in Sendai as a short term missionary to teach at Tohoku Gakuin, assist in evangelistic work and in the distribution of Church World Service Relief shipments from America. He was the first missionary to Japan from the Evangelical side of his denomination.

In 1951 he returned to the United States, spending one semester studying at New College in Edinburgh, Scotland. From 1952 to 1955 he studied at Union Theological Seminary and Columbia University in New York City, where he received his Ph. D. in 1957. His field was Social Ethics and Ecumenics, and the title of his dissertation under Dr. Searle Bates was, "The Protestant Missionary Understanding of the Missionary Message and Mission and the Chinese Situation from 1890 to 1911." In 1959 he married Barbara Dunn, daughter of Dr. David Dunn who then was Professor of Church History and Dean of Lancaster Theological Seminary. They have three children, Jeffrey, 1961, Martha, 1963, and Kathryn, 1967.

In 1964 the Mensendieks returned to Japan, and after language study in Tokyo were appointed to Tohoku Gakuin. In 1972 Dr. Mensendiek published "A Man for His Times, the Life and Thought of David B. Schneder." In 1975-76 he was Visiting Professor of Missions at the Pacific School of Religion in Berkeley, California, and in 1982-83, Visiting Scholar at Union Theological Seminary in New York City. In 1975 Eden Theological Seminary conferred upon him the honorary degree of Doctor of Divinity. Dr. Mensendiek has travelled widely, especially in Asia, visiting a wide variety of Christian institution and conferring both with missionaries and national Christians.

INDEX

A - Anti-Christian, 40, 49, 111, 113, 127, 140, 162, 185, 198, 204-205.

Anti-foreign, 111, 183, 185, 192, 198, 203-204.

Anti-missionary, 102, 113-117, 160-161, 185.

Apple, Dr. Thomas, 14, 87, 150.

Ault, Mary, 10, 11, 15, 17, 20, 34, 37, 39, 40, 51, 52.

Ault Memorial, 67, 68, 71-73, 78, 101.

B - Ballagh, 20-22, 23.

Baptisms, 19, 21, 39, 60, 99, 166, 173, 191.

Baptists, 8, 25, 26, 127.

Bartholomew, (Bd. Sec.) 56, 57, 74, 79, 80, 83, 92, 95, 207.

Bible women, 19, 128, 140, 143.

Boys' School, 10, 20, 22, 25, 32, 34, 35, 36. (cf. Sendai Theological Training School & Tohoku Gakuin).

Brown, Dr. Samuel, 21.

Buddhists, 60, 106, 119, 120, 141, 169, 171, 195.

C - Callender, (Bd. Sec.) 95, 97, 98, 125, 136.

China, 170-171, 173, 181-200.

China Mission, 188, 190, 193, 208, 212, 216.

Confucianism, 195.

Congregationalists, 9, 35, 36, 41, 44, 61, 78, 127, 197.

D - Debt, 92, 98, 151, 158-159.

DeForest, 36, 41, 50, 127.

Dutch Reformed Church, 9, 10, 16, 20, 21, 27, 59, 172.

E - Education, 10, 14, 17, 23, 31, 34, 41, 44, 47, 74, 132, 135, 151, 177, 212.

English, 18, 21, 25, 32, 34, 39, 40, 47, 50, 51, 54, 68, 77, 80, 126, 212.

Evangelicalism, 7, 8, 12.

Evangelism, 17, 18, 19, 22, 25, 34, 42-44, 55, 60, 61, 99, 106, 107, 120, 121, 129, 130, 151, 161, 177, 188, 191.

Evangelistic trips, 17, 22, 119-121, 165, 166-167, 185.

F - Female education, 10, 20, 25, 45, 59, 115-116, 165.

Ferris Seminary, 38, 59, 66.

Finances, 17, 44, 45, 52, 53, 55, 60, 67, 69, 72, 74, 76, 81, 82, 83, 87-88, 93, 94, 96, 97, 99, 106, 137, 150, 171, 193.

Financial problems, 17, 35, 48, 56, 72, 79, 122-125, 127, 134 -135, 164, 192.

Foreign Mission Board of Ref. Ch., 8, 10, 13, 23, 26, 34, 35, 37, 45, 47, 65, 66, 68, 69, 71, 75-78, 82-84, 86, 88, 92, 93, 95, 97, 98, 100, 101, 122, 124, 125, 150, 173, 181.

Franklin & Marshall College, 5-6, 14, 18, 61, 128, 149-150, 194, 197.

G - Gerhard, 100, 168, 200, 211.

Girls' School, 10, 20, 25, 38-40, 44, 47, 48, 52, 56, 65, 68, 73, 79, 95, 113, 139, 168, 169. (cf. Miyagi Gakuin).

Gring, 8, 10, 16, 17, 18, 19, 20, 22, 23, 24, 26, 27, 34, 35, 53, 82.

"Gring problem." 54, 70, 74-78, 83-88.

H - Heathen, 9, 25, 30, 31, 56, 60, 61, 141, 142, 168, 171, 189.

Hollowell, 99, 124, 174.

Home Church, (Ger. Ref.) 97, 99, 104, 122, 123, 144, 170, 172, 179, 181, 197, 207.

Housing, 17, 29, 38, 39, 51, 56-58, 66, 73, 186, 187.

Hoy - children, 80, 95, 103, 104, 128, 142, 143, 151, 168, 186, 189, 190, 196, 197, 198, 200, 208.

    conflict with Bd., 32, 55, 65, 71, 79, 92-99, 100-102, 122-125, 135-138, 144-145, 184.

    furloughs, 142, 143, 148-151, 197, 200-201.

    Gertrude, 128, 190, 197, 206, 208, 210, 211.

    gifts to mission, 67, 70, 96, 101.

    illnesses, 51, 56-58, 103, 118, 170, 184, 206.

    Mary, 137, 142, 143, 144, 147, 163, 168, 186, 187, 189, 200, 201, 207, 208-209.

    Robbery, 59, 163-165, 187.

I - Industrial Home, 126, 146, 150, 158.

Iwanuma church, 22, 34.

J - Japan Evangelist, 142-143, 144, 147, 148, 168, 173, 176.

Japan Mission of Reformed Church, 17, 27, 47, 65, 70, 71, 75-78, 81, 83, 88, 93, 109, 118, 140, 146, 158, 159, 170, 171, 172, 175, 212.

Japanese control of Mission, 39, 41, 68-71, 93, 112-117, 127, 140, 145, 147, 159-162, 315.

    government recognition, 16, 32, 39, 106.

        schools, 44, 127, 132.

        support, 36, 162.

Ministry of Education, 48, 162.

nationalism, 102, 111, 113, 116, 140, 160, 161, 169.

K – Kelker (Board treasurer), 10, 36, 42, 50, 59, 66, 67, 74, 76, 77, 78, 84, 86, 92, 93, 95, 98, 106, 118, 136, 147.

Kami, 33, 134, 152.

Kaneko, 14, 149-150, 159.

L – Lancaster, 4, 5, 6-7, 18, 19, 137, 149-150, 207.

Lancaster Seminary, 5, 12, 14, 18, 33, 87, 95, 149, 207, 212.

M – Messenger, 4, 10, 13, 24, 29, 30, 34, 35, 38, 47, 55, 56, 72, 81, 82, 83, 84, 85, 86, 87, 93, 94, 95, 96, 98, 108, 126, 133, 134, 141, 148, 162, 164, 166, 171, 182, 188, 192, 197.

Methodists, 10, 18, 25, 26, 127, 182, 187, 191.

Mifflinburg, 1, 13, 80, 151, 191, 198, 207.

Miller, Henry, 128, 165, 174.

Missionary Guardian, 106, 119, 135, 142.

Miyagi Classis, 55, 68, 81, 159-161.

Miyagi Gakuin, 39, 40, 47, 51, 165, 212, 215. (cf. Girls' School).

Moore, 8, 11, 16, 18, 19, 23, 24, 26, 27, 34, 53, 54, 74, 83, 98, 111, 142, 165, 174.

Music, 51, 55, 68, 99.

N – Nagamachi Church, 99, 130, 167, 173.

Niigata, 21, 22.

Niijima, 36, 41.

Noss, 162, 172, 174, 176, 200.

O – Oshikawa, 19, 20, 21, 22-23, 26-27, 32, 36, 44, 60, 72, 77, 78, 80, 81-83, 94, 102, 108, 112, 114-117, 126, 133, 135, 139, 140, 145, 146, 147, 150, 151, 158, 159, 160, 161, 162, 163, 175.

P - Poems, 152-155, 177-179.

Poorbaugh, Emma, 62, 117, 139.

Kittie, 11, 37, 45, 50, 140.

Lizzie, 10, 11, 16, 20, 34, 37, 38, 48, 49, 58, 70, 74, 113-115, 139.

Presbyterians, 9, 16, 19, 27, 124.

R - Roman Catholics, 22, 26, 52, 127, 192.

S - Scholarships, 68, 82, 97, 99-100.

Schneder, 6, 13, 56, 59, 61, 67, 70, 74, 83, 87-88, 94, 108, 112, 130, 139, 140, 141, 146, 148, 158, 165, 169, 171, 172, 174, 194, 206, 210.

Schwartz, 26, 57-58.

Sendai Church, 22, 25, 59, 60, 67, 96, 148, 165, 169.

Sendai Theological Training School, 34, 60, 67, 68, 72, 76-77, 81, 86-88, 97, 100, 101, 105, 118, 119. (cf. Boys' School & Tohoku Gakuin).

Shiroishi Church, 43-44, 60, 99.

Sunday Schools, 10, 12, 17, 51, 99, 128, 130.

T - Takayama, 96, 104-105, 186.

Tohoku Gakuin, 97, 106-108, 125-126, 132, 134, 135, 138, 145, 147, 148, 158, 161, 163, 165, 168, 175, 200, 215. (cf. Boys' School & Sendai Theological Training School).

Toka School, 36, 41, 44, 54, 127.

Tokyo, 17, 21, 24, 26, 35, 37, 53, 76, 97, 137, 162, 165, 174, 175.

U - Union Church, 27, 37, 43, 55, 61, 67, 68, 69, 85, 86, 159-160.

Union Seminary, 20, 85, 191.

W - Women, position of, 35, 44, 114, 116, 126, 137, 171, 189, 195-196.

Y - Yamagata, 43, 54, 56, 59, 72, 77, 83, 165, 174, 200.

Yochow, Boys' School, 191.

Girls' School, 189, 190.

Yokohama, 16, 17, 20, 21, 38, 59, 65, 125, 118, 137, 143, 206.

Yokohama Band, 21, 39.

Yoshida Kametaro, 22, 165-166, 175.

Misao, 19, 128-130, 143, 149, 151.